~SPURGEON~

The Triumph of Faith in a Believer's Life

CLC
CHRISTIAN ~ LIVING ~ CLASSICS

CHARLES SPURGEON
CHRISTIAN LIVING CLASSICS

Grace Abounding in a Believer's Life

A Passion for Holiness in a Believer's Life

The Power of Prayer in a Believer's Life

Spiritual Warfare in a Believer's Life

The Triumph of Faith in a Believer's Life

What the Holy Spirit Does in a Believer's Life

CHARLES SPURGEON
Christian Living Classics

The Triumph of Faith in a Believer's Life

Compiled and Edited by ROBERT HALL

Emerald Books

P.O. Box 635 • Lynnwood, Washington 98046

Scripture quotations are taken from the King James Version of the Bible

The Triumph of Faith in a Believer's Life
Copyright © 1994
Lance C. Wubbels

Published by Emerald Books
P.O. Box 635
Lynnwood, WA 98046

ISBN 1-883002-08-7

Printed in the United States of America

To

Eric Burgdorf

"He was a

faithful man,

and feared God

above many."

About the Editor

ROBERT HALL is the pseudonym for Lance Wubbels, the managing editor of Bethany House Publishers. His interest in the writings of Charles Spurgeon began while doing research on an editorial project that required extensive reading of Spurgeon's sermons. He discovered a wealth of sermon classics that are filled with practical, biblical insight for every believer and written in a timeless manner that makes them as relevant today as the day they were spoken. His desire is to select and present Spurgeon's writings in a way that will appeal to a wide audience of readers and allow one of the greatest preachers of all time to enrich believers' lives.

About the Author

CHARLES HADDON SPURGEON (1834–1892) was the remarkable British "Boy Preacher of the Fens" who became one of the truly greatest preachers of all time. Coming from a flourishing country pastorate in 1854, he accepted a call to pastor London's New Park Street Chapel. This building soon proved too small and so work on Spurgeon's Metropolitan Tabernacle was begun in 1859. Meanwhile his weekly sermons were being printed and having a remarkable sale—25,000 copies every week in 1865 and translated into more than twenty languages.

Spurgeon built the Metropolitan Tabernacle into a congregation of over 6,000 and added well over 14,000 members during his thirty-eight-year London ministry. The combination of his clear voice, his mastery of language, his sure grasp of Scripture, and a deep love for Christ produced some of the noblest preaching of any age. An astounding 3,561 sermons have been preserved in sixty-three volumes, *The New Park Street Pulpit* and *The Metropolitan Tabernacle Pulpit*, from which the chapters of this book have been selected and edited.

During his lifetime, Spurgeon is estimated to have preached to 10,000,000 people. He remains history's most widely read preacher. There is more available material written by Spurgeon than by any other Christian author, living or dead. His sixty-three volumes of sermons stand as the largest set of books by a single author in the history of Christianity, comprising the equivalent to the twenty-seven volumes of the ninth edition of the *Encyclopedia Britannica*.

Contents

Introduction

WHEN IT COMES TO THE MOST VITAL and personal relationship in life—a Christian's faith in Jesus Christ—it is almost certain there will be questions and wonderings. Yet most people feel uncomfortable asking those questions out loud for fear that their commitment to Christ will be questioned in return. When faced with a challenge like this, there's nothing like wise advice from a friend who's "been there." And when it comes to understanding the powerful role of faith in a believer's life, I know of few men more qualified to teach or preach on it than Charles Spurgeon.

Considered by his peers then and now as "The Prince of Preachers," Charles Spurgeon built London's Metropolitan Tabernacle into the world's largest independent congregation during the nineteenth century. During his remarkable thirty-eight-year ministry, no building in London seemed big enough to house all those who wanted to hear him preach. Spurgeon was noted as a passionate biblical expositor of the gospel who spoke the language of the common people and met them at the point of their deepest needs.

Well over one hundred years have gone by since Spurgeon's voice echoed through that great London church, but time has in no way diminished the powerful effect of Spurgeon's recorded sermons. They live on through the printed page and are as relevant today as the day on which he preached them. Because he was so thoroughly grounded in biblical doctrine and so insightful into the human condition, his messages bear a timeless trait that supersedes the era in which they were given and inspires and transforms listeners in any age.

As a gifted and powerful evangelist, there was nothing that so preoccupied Spurgeon's thinking and preaching as helping his listeners come to a personal experience of faith in Jesus Christ. For Charles Spurgeon, the foundation of the Christian faith, the victory and joy of faith, the life and walk of faith, all revolved around the person of Jesus Christ. This he made clear in one of his early sermons at the New Park Street Church. He declared:

> Jesus is *the truth*. We believe in *Him*—*not merely* his words. *He* himself is Doctor and Doctrine, Revealer and Revelation, the Illuminator and Light of Men. He is exalted in every word of truth, because he is its sum and substance . . . Sermons are valuable in proportion as they speak *of* Him and point *to him*. A Christless gospel is no gospel and a Christless discourse is the cause of merriment to devils.

This characterized Spurgeon's preaching throughout his eminently successful ministry. He preached Christ very practically, and thus he preached a practical Christian faith. One is hard pressed to find any sermon where Jesus Christ was not presented and extolled and practical applications to faith made to Spurgeon's congregation.

And Spurgeon was well aware of the tendency of human nature to doubt rather than to believe. Observing those he ministered to weekly, he commented:

> I know people who seem to be always shaping fresh nets of doubt to get entangled in. Like mariners who seek the rocks or soldiers who court the point of a bayonet, this is unprofitable business. Practically, morally, mentally, and spiritually, doubting is an evil trade. Doubt is sterile, a desert without water. Doubt discovers difficulties that it never solves and creates hesitancy, despondency, despair. Its progress is the decay of comfort, the death of peace. *Believe* is the word that speaks life into a man, but doubt nails down his coffin. I entreat you to look up and see the pierced hands and feet and side of the dear Redeemer. Read eternal mercy and full forgiveness there, and then go your way in peace, for you are well pleasing to God. He will receive you graciously and love you freely. Come to

Him, for He is the rewarder of them that diligently seek him.

Spurgeon also observed the tendency in believers to be defeated by running away from the trials of their faith. Rather than seizing their faith as a spiritual shield that would triumph over doubts and trials, Spurgeon noted:

> Some Christians think that faith should enable them to escape the blows—that if they had faith, everything would be peaceful and calm. They think they are going to ride softly to heaven, singing all the way. Why do they put their armor on at all if they are to have no battles? Why enlist if you are not to fight? No, let the soldier be ready when war comes; let him expect the conflict as a part and necessary consequence of his profession. But be armed with faith; it receives the blows. The poor shield is knocked and hammered and battered like a house exposed in a time of storm. Blow after blow comes rattling upon it, and though it turns death aside, yet the shield is compelled itself to hear the cut and the thrust. So must our faith do—it must be cut at, it must bear the blows.

Every believer in Jesus Christ must wrestle and fight for issues of faith in his life. To believe with certainty that God speaks truth is where Satan and the powers of darkness rage against the believer in the strongest manner, and to concede defeat in a matter of faith is devastating. It is of utmost importance, then, that a Christian make sure that he understands what faith is and how it is personally obtained. And he must understand what it means to walk by faith and without sight, how faith is tried and triumphs, how faith is made effective as it works through love, and how faith can see God's glory.

I invite you to read these twelve select chapters on faith as you would listen to a trusted and skilled pastor. There is nothing speculative about Spurgeon's teaching; just the rock-solid truth. Spurgeon will meet you where you live, and you will not be disappointed.

Careful editing has helped to sharpen the focus of these sermons while retaining the authentic and timeless flavor they undoubtedly bring.

Regarding Him as the Son of the Highest, we see an overwhelming argument for faith, for who can doubt the merit of that work that begins with the holy Son lying prostrate in Gethsemane, exceeding sorrowful, even unto death. Then, we trace Him as He is seized by His captors and hurried to the high priest, to Herod, and to Pilate. How they pour contempt upon Him! How the smiters scourge Him! How the abjects mock Him! His lowest shame, His worst desertion, His bitterest griefs, His dying pangs all say to us, "Cannot you trust Him?" Then comes the death scene. With tears in our eyes we stand at the cross and see those blessed hands and feet nailed to the tree that He might be made a curse for us. Can unbelief live after this? Before His heart is opened by the spear thrust, we see Him bleeding in every part of His body and soul, for He is a mass of anguish. Of His suffering, we dare not speak, for they are of a depth that no plumbline can ever fathom. O Son of God, if ever it were treason to doubt Your power to save, it must be so when we see You hanging upon the cross. You have triumphed over our unbelief upon the bloody tree. Now you lead our captivity captive, and we bow before You, fully assured that You are mighty to save. We feel constrained to cry, "I must believe. Those nails have crucified my unbelief. That spear has slain my doubts."

Chapter One

Faith's Sure Foundation

He that believeth on him shall not be confounded—1 Peter 2:6.

THE VERSE FROM PETER gives a remarkable insight into the foundation of our faith. It is a passage that was a favorite quotation with the apostles and worthy of our serious consideration. If you turn to the Epistle to the Romans, you will find Paul quoting it again and again in rapid succession (Romans 9:33; 10:11). It is a quotation from Isaiah 28:16, where we find it written: "Therefore thus saith the Lord GOD, Behold, I lay in Zion for a foundation a stone, a tried stone, a precious corner stone, a sure foundation: he that believeth shall not make haste." Paul interprets that as "shall not be ashamed," and Peter renders it as "shall not be confounded." From the variation of the translations we obtain two or three different shades of meaning, all derived from the same thing. The sentence seemed to the Holy Spirit to be so full, so complete, and so forcible that He repeated it often. The harp is a choice one; let us play upon it, and let our ears drink in the melody: "He that believeth on him shall not be condemned."

The Foundation of Our Faith

The foundation of the believer's faith is Jesus Christ. "He that believeth on *him*." The believer receives doctrine because Christ has taught it, but it is not a doctrine but a person who is the foundation of his confidence. The apostle does not say, "I know *what* I have believed," though that would be true, but he does say, "I know *whom* I have believed, and am persuaded that he is able to keep that which I have committed unto him against that day" (2 Tim. 1:12). The faith that saves the soul is confidence in a Person, reliance upon One who will certainly effect the salvation of those who trust Him.

In what sense am I to believe in Jesus Christ? Under what aspects does the believer rest in Christ? I reply, first, *as God's appointed Savior of men.* Mark what the Lord says in Isaiah: "Behold, I lay in Zion a sure foundation." We trust in Jesus Christ because God has set Him forth to be the propitiation for sin. When sin first came into the world, God in tender mercy gave our parents the first promise concerning the seed of the woman who would bruise the serpent's head. We believe Jesus of Nazareth is that seed of the woman, and we trust in Him to bruise the serpent's head on our behalf. Promises were multiplied as the ages went on, and Jesus was set forth under various types and figures but always as the Messiah who would deliver ruined souls. All those promises and prophecies are fulfilled in Jesus Christ the Son of God. Since God appoints Him as a Savior, we accept Him as a Savior. We believe the apostolic witness by the mouth of John: "And we have seen and do testify that the Father sent the Son to be the Saviour of the world" (1 John 4:14). This is the great stronghold of our confidence that gives us peace with God.

We also believe in the Lord Jesus because of *the excellency of His person.* We trust Christ to save us because we perceive Him in every way to be adapted by the nature and constitution of His Person to be the Savior of mankind. It was needful that the Savior of men should be a man. A man had broken the law, and a man must keep it, for only the obedience of man could answer the requirements of the law. By the sin of a man we became subject to punishment, and only by the sufferings of a man could the law be vindicated. It is with gladness that we read that the Son of God became a partaker of flesh and blood and came under the law. Born of a virgin, He was wrapped in swaddling clothes like any other child. He grew in stature as other children do and lived with His parents until the time of His revealing. "The Word was made flesh, and dwelt among us, (and we beheld his glory, the glory as of the only begotten of the Father,) full of grace and truth" (John 1:14). He labored and suffered and died among us. He was really a man, but all the while a perfect Man without a trace of fault. Thus He was able to fulfill the perfect law of God on our behalf. We rejoice as we see that Jesus is our next of kin to whom the right of redemption belongs, the perfect Man, the second Adam of our race.

Yet more confident are we because we see that His manhood is in union with deity. We subscribe to the ancient church confession: "He is very God of very God." In no diminished sense, but with the strongest emphasis that can be put upon words, we believe Him to be "over all, God blessed for ever" (Rom. 9:5). He is "Emmanuel, which being interpreted is, God with us" (Matt. 1:23). We salute Him as "My Lord and my God" (John 20:28). We perceive that His deity must have put an infinite merit into the sufferings of His humanity and that because He was God He was able to undertake the stupendous labor of our redemption. His holy life and suffering death are, because of His Godhead, fully equal to the redemption of the vast multitudes who by Him do believe in God who raised Him from the dead. We see Jesus to be completely equipped for His work, divinely strong yet humanly compassionate, eternally existing as God and yet capable of death because He was encompassed with a human body. O thou glorious One, whose name is fitly called Wonderful, my soul cannot imagine a Savior in whom I could confide with so much ease. It seems but natural to us who are believers to rest in such a person as He, who can with one hand touch the Godhead and yet with the other hand embrace our nature.

Another ground of our reliance upon Christ is that *He has actually finished the work of our redemption*. There are two things to be done. The first was the keeping of the law on our behalf. That Christ performed to the uttermost, even as He said to His Father, "I have glorified thee on the earth: I have finished the work which thou gavest me to do" (John 17:4). We read the four gospels with delight and perceive the exceeding beauties of His matchless character. For innocence, He is spotless as a lily; for zeal, He is red as the rose. There was no fault in our Beloved. He is a lamb without blemish and without spot. He fulfills both tables of the law and presents to God a perfect righteousness on our behalf. When the Lord presents that righteousness of Christ to us that it may be set to our account, we feel the blessedness of the man to whom the Lord imputes righteousness without works, and we are exceeding glad.

We see our Lord also doing the other part of His work, namely, suffering in consequence of our sin. We must accompany our Lord to the garden of Gethsemane. There every drop of blood pleads with us that we should trust Him. There His sighs and cries and throes of anguish all plead with us that we should rely upon Him. Regarding Him as the Son of the Highest, we see an overwhelming argument for faith, for who can doubt the merit of that work that begins with the holy Son lying prostrate in Gethsemane, exceeding sorrowful, even unto death. Then, we trace Him as He is seized by His captors and hurried to the high priest, to Herod, and to Pilate. How they pour contempt upon Him! How the smiters scourge Him! How the abjects mock Him! His lowest shame, His worst desertion, His bitterest griefs, His dying pangs all say to us, "Cannot you trust Him?" Then comes the death scene. With tears in our eyes we stand at the cross and see those blessed hands and feet nailed to the tree that He might be made a curse for us. Can unbelief live after this? Before His heart is opened by the spear thrust, we see Him bleeding in every part of His body and soul, for He is a mass of anguish. Of His suffering, we dare not speak, for they are of a depth that no plumbline can ever fathom. O Son of God, if ever it were treason to doubt Your power to save, it must be so when we see You hanging upon the cross. You have triumphed over our unbelief upon the bloody tree. Now you lead our captivity captive, and we bow before You, fully assured that You are mighty to save. We feel constrained to cry, "I must believe. Those nails have crucified my unbelief. That spear has slain my doubts." It is upon the sufferings of our Lord Jesus that we rely for our cleansing: "the chastisement of our peace was upon him; and with his stripes we are healed" (Isa. 53:5).

Seeing that our Lord is no longer dead, we also find it easier to put our confidence in Him because *He ever liveth to see to the completion of our salvation*. A living faith delights in a living Savior. This is the seal of all that went before. He must have made an end of sin and brought in everlasting righteousness or else He would not be sitting at the right hand of the Father, crowned with glory and honor. That one sacrifice that our High Priest offered upon Calvary has put away all the sin of His people forever. There is, therefore, no need of a repetition of it. "But this man, after he had offered one sacrifice for sins for ever, sat down on the right hand of God" (Heb. 10:12).

The righteousness with which we are clothed is completely woven, the fountain in which we are washed is completely filled, and now no one can condemn those who believe in Jesus. "It is finished" has ended every accusation. Jesus has gone to heaven before us as our representative and is preparing a place for us. When the time shall come for us to climb to our thrones, nothing may be lacking to complete our joys. Meanwhile He is pleading the merit of His blood on behalf of all who trust Him. And He is working by His unseen Spirit to preserve His own from every temptation and to keep them and to perfect them that they may be presented faultless before His presence with exceeding great joy. "Wherefore he is able also to save them to the uttermost that come unto God by him, seeing he ever liveth to make intercession for them" (Heb. 7:25).

Such is the sure foundation of our faith. For these most sufficient reasons we trust ourselves with the Redeemer. This we do with all sincerity and deliberation, believing that these reasons will bear examination and are such as none need to be ashamed of.

The Manner of This Believing

How do we believe in Jesus Christ? Return to Peter's instructive thought: "Behold, I lay in Zion a chief corner stone, elect, precious: and he that believeth on him shall not be confounded." If we were to carry out the idea, it would run: "He that is built upon Christ shall not be removed." We can most naturally understand the laying of a stone upon the foundation to be suggested as a description of faith. To believe on Jesus is to *lie upon Him as a stone lies upon the foundation* when the mason put it there. There is the foundation firm and strong, a precious cornerstone, tried and sure. Here is a smaller stone, quarried from the pit, and the builder places it upon the foundation. Its lying on the foundation represents faith. Our souls' eternal interests are laid on Christ. The foundation bears up the stone and holds it in place; so Christ bears up our souls and holds them in place so as not to fall to the ground. Faith is leaning, depending, relying, casting all care upon Him. Faith is the giving up of self-reliance and independence and the resting of the soul upon Him whom God has laid in Zion for a foundation.

A stone rests wholly on the foundation. Resting upon Christ means wholly looking to Him for everything that has to do with our salvation. Genuine faith in Christ does not trust *Him* to pardon sin and then trust *itself* to overcome sin. It trusts Christ for both. We must depend upon the Lord to keep us to the end just as we do for pardon from the past. We rejoice in a Savior who promises to keep us as long as we keep ourselves. There must be no reliance for us but upon Christ for all things—wisdom, righteousness, sanctification, ultimate perfection. We are complete in Christ and can add no perfection to Him.

It is when we fail to rest upon Christ that our souls run into trouble. Some of us try to build little wooden platforms of our own experience onto the foundation. Some build them so high that they talk about being perfect or very near to it. These wooden affairs shake with a little extra weight and make people tremble. Get down upon the Rock as low as you can and simply grasp it. Rest on the everlasting love of Jesus, and you will be safe.

The stone laid on the foundation comes closer to that foundation every day. "To whom coming," says Peter, "as unto a living stone" (1 Pet. 2:4). When a house is finished, there still occurs a degree of settling, and you are glad if it settles all in a piece together. Every day the stone is brought by its own weight a little closer to the foundation. May every day's pressures bring you closer to Christ.

A well-built stone gets to be one with the foundation. In the old Roman walls, the mortar seems to be as hard as the stones, and the whole is like one piece. So it is with the believer, who rests upon the Lord until he grows up into Him, till he is one with Jesus by a living union, so that you hardly know where the foundation ends and the building begins.

"But I thought I had to do something for my salvation," you say. Does the stone do anything to maintain its position beyond lying in its place? Your strength is to sit still and rest in the Lord. There is plenty for you to do for your Lord to show your love to Him and to glorify His name. But you cannot add to the foundation of your confidence and should never dream of trying. How could you improve on what your Lord declares to be finished? The more you lean upon Jesus, the better He will be pleased. "Lean hard," He cries, "and prove your love to Me." Trust Him in life and in death and to eternity, and you will not be ashamed or confounded.

The Reward of Faith

The text reads: "He shall not be confounded," and the meaning of it is, first, that he shall never be *disappointed*. All that Christ has promised to be He will be to those who trust Him. If Christ is the promised Savior, He will surely save. He does not begin to build and then walk away because of a lack of supplies. He will keep the believer, support the believer, and perfect the believer. You will never have to say of Christ, "Well, there is much good in Him, but not as much as I expected." Even inspiration itself could not tell us so completely that we could fully understand how sweet, how excellent, how sure, how full our Lord is. We know His love, but it "passeth knowledge" (Eph. 3:19). The grand truth is that the believer shall never have any cause to be ashamed of Jesus. Believers shall never be driven to confess that they made a mistake in trusting Him. The most childlike confidence in God in Christ Jesus is nothing more than He deserves. It is always the highest wisdom to place all in His hands and leave it there for time and eternity. To risk all with Jesus is to end all risk. Faith is safe as the throne of the Eternal.

Another rendering indicates that we will never be *confounded*. When a man gets to be ashamed of his hope because of disappointment, he casts about for another anchor and, not knowing where to look, is in a greatly perplexed state. If the Lord Jesus Christ were to fall through, where would we go? There is no other person in whom we may confide. There are many religions on the face of the earth, but none of them bears as much comparison to our faith as a candle to the sun. They are all hollow mockeries, offering nothing that satisfies the hungry heart. Lord, to whom should we go if we should turn from you? Whither could we fly? If wisdom is not in You, where shall we search for it? "The depth saith, It is not in me: and the sea saith, It is not with me" (Job 28:14). There is no ransom from wrath if this redemption price is null and void. No. In Jesus we shall not be confounded, for we shall never be disappointed in Him!

According to Isaiah's version (28:16) we shall not be obliged to *make haste*. We shall not be driven to our wits' end and hurry to and fro. We shall not worry and fret and fume, trying this and that, running from pillar to post to seek a hope. He that believes shall be quiet, calm, collected, assured, confident. He awaits the future with a steady calm as he endures the present with patience. See what a blessed promise this is to those who believe in Jesus.

There are special dangers of being confounded, but none of them need damage our faith. There are times when a man's sins all come up before him like exceeding great armies. It is a mighty easy thing to think that you are believing in Christ when you are not conscious of any great sin, but true faith is not confounded even when it groans under a grievous sense of sin. There are times when sins multiply and we cry with David, "For mine iniquities are gone over mine head, as a heavy burden they are too heavy for me" (Ps. 38:4). Have you ever had times in which all the ghosts of your dead and buried sins rise again and come marching upon you armed to the teeth? Suppose all the worst of your past rise at once, what would become of you? "He that believeth on him shall not be confounded." Though he sees the whole horde of his sins march by, the believer cries, "They are all gone into the tomb where Jesus slept, and the blood of Jesus has cleansed me. The depths have covered them. There is not one of them left. They sank like lead in the mighty waters, for God has cast them all into the depths of the sea."

The unbelieving world labors to create confusion. The gentlemen of higher criticism, the scientific discoverers, the possessors of boastful culture, and all the other braggers of the nineteenth century are up in arms against the believers in Jesus. Well, let all this wisdom of the world assail us! I protest that if all the sages of the world were to utter one thundering sarcasm, if they concentrated all their scorn into one universal sneer of contempt, I do not think it would now affect me the turn of a hair, so sure am I that my Lord will justify my confidence. "I know whom I have believed," and I also know that my Lord Jesus Christ "sitteth upon the flood; yea, the LORD sitteth King for ever" (Ps. 29:10). To trust the Son of God whose advent into this world is a fact better proved by history than any other that was ever on record is the most reasonable thing a person can do. There is nothing about our faith that demands an apology. We fling back in the teeth of the scoffer the charge of unreasoning dogmatism—ours is the most reasonable of all beliefs. We shall not be confounded by the world's foolishness.

But the world has done more than sneer. It has imitated Cain and sought to slay the faithful. The enemies of the gospel have raged against the church of God. Christ has seemed to say, "Come on, world. Here are My disciples whom you despise. Come and see if you can conquer them! I give you a fair opportunity. There is the Colosseum where you heap up tier upon tier of men and women with cruel eyes and savage hearts. Bring out the saints and cry, 'Christians, to the lions!' " There the faithful stand. Do they cry for mercy and deny Christ? They are but feeble men and women, but they die as bravely as any soldier fell in battle. The enemy resolves to try them with torture, with rack, and rod, and fire. Every form of possible cruelty has in later persecutions been tried, but believers have not been confounded. How the saints of the Lord clapped their burning hands and cried, "None but Christ!" while the flames devoured them. The enemy could not confound them. We cannot strike our adversaries, but by bearing their blows we shall, like the anvil, break the hammers.

There will come other troubles to Christians besides these, and in them they shall not be confounded. Believers shall be tried when the natural desires of the flesh break loose into vehement lustings, and corruptions will seek to cast them down. He who believes in Christ shall conquer himself and overcome his easily besetting sins. There will come losses and crosses, business trials and domestic bereavements. What then? The Lord shall sustain the believer under every tribulation. At last, death will come to us. Loved ones will wipe the cold sweat from our brows, and we shall gasp for breath, but we shall not be confounded then. We may not be able to shout "victory," but our last breath will echo the precious name of Jesus. They who watch us shall know by our serenity that a Christian does not die but only melts away into everlasting life. And we shall not be confounded as we pass into the grandeurs of eternity to stand before our Lord the Judge of all. We will tell the Father in that day that we have rested on the salvation that He appointed, that we have confided in His own dear Son, and that we believed that the blood of Jesus did make atonement for our sin. We shall not be confounded on that most solemn day.

We can never be confounded, because our salvation is completely based upon what God has said and who He is. No believer can ever be confounded until the Godhead itself shall be undeified. Until God the Father can break His word, He must do all that He has promised in Christ. Everything hangs upon the divine fidelity. But it shall never be and can never be. Because Jesus lives, we shall live also and not be confounded. Let us rest in our Lord's faithfulness and receive the pledges of His eternal affection.

*F*aith exists in various degrees according to the amount of knowledge or other causes. Sometimes faith is little more than a simple clinging to Christ in a sense of utter dependence. Thousands of God's people have no more faith than this. They know enough to cling to Jesus with all their heart and soul. Jesus Christ is to them a Savior strong and mighty, like an immovable and immutable rock. They cleave to Him for dear life, and this clinging saves them. God gives to His people the propensity to cling. Though this is a very simple sort of faith, it is a very complete and effectual form of it. In fact, it is the heart of all faith, and that to which we are often driven when we are in deep trouble or when our mind is somewhat bemuddled by sickness or depression in spirit. We can cling when we can do nothing else, and that is the very soul of faith. Always cling to what you know. If as yet you are only like a lamb that wades a little into the river of life and not like leviathan who stirs the mighty deep to the bottom, yet drink. For it is drinking and not diving that will save you. Cling to Jesus, for that is faith.

Chapter Two

Faith Defined and Obtained

For by grace are ye saved through faith; and that not of yourselves: it is the gift of God—Ephesians 2:8.

WHILE I PURPOSE TO DWELL upon the expression "through faith," I must first call attention to the fountainhead of our salvation: "by grace are ye saved." Because God is gracious, sinful men are forgiven, converted, purified, and saved. It is not because of anything in them or that ever can be in them. They are saved because of the boundless love, goodness, pity, compassion, mercy, and grace of God. Behold the pure river of water of life as it pours out of the throne of God and of the Lamb (Rev. 22:1). What an abyss is the grace of God. Who can fathom it. Like all of the divine attributes, it is infinite. God is full of love, for "God is love" (1 John 4:8). Unbounded goodness and love enter into the very essence of the Godhead.

It is because "his mercy endureth for ever" (Ps.106:1) that men are not destroyed and because "his compassions fail not" (Lam. 3:22) that sinners are brought to Himself and forgiven. Keep in mind, then, that grace is the fountain and source of faith itself. Faith is the work of God's grace in us. No one can say that Jesus is the Christ but by the Holy Spirit (1 Cor. 12:3). "No man can come to me [Christ], except the Father which hath sent me draw him" (John

6:44). So that faith, which is coming to Christ, is the result of divine drawing. Grace is the first and last moving cause of salvation, and faith, important as it is, is only an important part of the work that grace employs.

Grace is the fountain and the stream. Faith is the channel or aqueduct along which the flood of mercy flows down to refresh the thirsty sons of men. It is a tremendous pity when the aqueduct is broken. The sight of the broken aqueducts around Rome that no longer convey water into the city is picturesque. Even so, faith must be kept true and sound, leading right up to God and coming right down to ourselves, that it may become a serviceable channel of mercy to our souls. Still, let me remind you that faith must not be exalted above the divine source of all blessing that lies in the grace of God. Never make a Christ of your faith or think of it as if it were an independent source of your salvation. Our life is found in "looking unto Jesus" (Heb. 12:2), not in looking to our own faith. By faith all things become possible to us, yet the power is not in the faith but in the God upon whom faith relies.

Grace is the locomotive, and faith is the chain by which the carriage of the soul is attached to the great motive power. The righteousness of faith is not the moral excellence of faith but the righteousness of Jesus Christ that faith grasps and appropriates. The peace within the soul is not derived from the contemplation of our faith. It comes from Him who is our peace, the hem of whose garment faith touches and virtue comes out of Him into the soul. It is a very important thing, however, that we consider the channel and that the Holy Spirit shall help us to understand it. Faith, *what is it?* Faith, *why is it selected as the channel of blessing?* Faith, *how can it be obtained and increased?*

What Is Faith?

There are many descriptions of faith, but almost all the definitions I have read have made me understand it less. Faith is the simplest of all things, and perhaps because of its simplicity it is more difficult to explain.

Faith is made up of three things: knowledge, belief, and trust. Knowledge comes first. Some people hold that a man can believe what he does not know, but I cannot. "How shall they believe in him of whom they have not heard?" (Rom. 10:14). I want to be informed of a fact before I can possibly believe it. "Faith cometh by hearing" (Rom. 10:17). We must first hear in order to know what we are to believe. "They that know thy name will put their trust in thee" (Ps. 9:10). A degree of knowledge is essential to faith. "Incline your ear, and come unto me: hear, and your soul shall live" (Isa. 55:3)—such was the word of the ancient prophet, and it is the word of the gospel still. Search the Scriptures and learn what the Holy Spirit teaches concerning Christ and His salvation. Seek to know God: "that he is, and that he is a rewarder of them that diligently seek him" (Heb. 11:6). Know what the good news of the gospel is, how it talks of free forgiveness and change of heart, of adoption into the family of God, and of countless other blessings. And know especially Christ Jesus the Son of God, the Savior of men, united to us by His human nature and united to God, seeing He is divine. Jesus is able to act as mediator between God and man, able to lay His hand upon both and to be the connecting link between the sinner and the Judge of all the earth.

Endeavor to know more and more of Christ. After Paul had been converted over twenty years, he writes the Philippians that he desired to know Christ (Phil. 3:10). Depend upon it that the more we know of Jesus, the more we shall wish to know of Him. Endeavor especially to know the doctrine of the sacrifice of Christ, for this is the center of the target at which faith aims. Saving faith fixes itself upon the fact that "God was in Christ, reconciling the world unto himself, not imputing their trespasses unto them" (2 Cor. 5:19). Know that Jesus was made a curse for us, as it is written: "Cursed is every one that hangeth on a tree" (Gal. 3:13). Drink deep into the doctrine of the substitutionary work of Christ, for therein lies the sweetest possible comfort to the guilty sons of men, since the Lord "made him to be sin for us . . . that we might be made the righteousness of God in him" (2 Cor. 5:21). Faith, then, begins with knowledge of divine truth.

The mind goes on to *believe* that these things are true. The soul believes that God hears the cries of sincere hearts, that the gospel is from God, and that justification by faith is the grand truth that God has revealed by His Spirit. Then the heart believes that Jesus is truly our God and Savior, the Redeemer of men, the Prophet,

Priest, and King of His people. Get firmly to believe that "the blood of Jesus Christ his Son cleanseth us from all sin" (1 John 1:7). Jesus' sacrifice is complete and fully accepted of God on man's behalf.

One more ingredient is needed to complete faith, and that is *trust*. Commit yourself to the merciful God. Rest your hope on the gracious gospel. Trust your soul on the dying and living Savior. Wash away your sins in the atoning blood. Accept His perfect righteousness. Trust is the lifeblood of faith, and there is no saving faith without it. Cast yourself totally upon Christ, rest in Him, commit yourself to Him. That done, you have exercised saving faith. Faith is not a blind thing, for faith begins with knowledge. It is not a speculative thing, for faith believes facts of which it is sure. It is not an impractical, dreamy thing, for faith stakes its eternal destiny upon the truth of revelation. Faith *ventures* its all upon the truth of God.

If my description of faith confuses you, let me try again. *Faith is believing that Christ is who He is said to be, that He will do what He has promised to do, and expecting this of Him.* The Scriptures speak of Jesus Christ as being God in human flesh, as being perfect in His character, as being made a sin offering on our behalf, as bearing sins in His body on the tree. Scripture speaks of Him as having finished transgression, made an end of sin, and brought in everlasting righteousness. The Scriptures further tell us that He "rose again," that He "ever liveth to make intercession for them" (Heb. 7:25), that He has gone up into glory and has taken possession of heaven on the behalf of His people, and that He will come again "to judge the earth . . . with righteousness . . . and the people with equity" (Ps. 98:9). We are most firmly to believe that this is so, for we have the testimony of God the Father when He said, "This is my beloved Son: hear him" (Luke 9:35). This also is testified by God the Holy Spirit, for the Spirit has borne witness to Christ, both by the word and by miracles and by His working in the hearts of men. We are to believe this testimony to be true.

Faith also believes that Christ will do what He has promised. If Christ has promised to cast out none that come to Him, it is certain that He will not cast us out if we come to Him (John 6:37). Faith believes that if Jesus said, "The water that I shall give him shall be in him a well of water springing up into everlasting life" (John 4:14), it must be true. If we get this living water from Christ, it will abide in us and well up within us in streams of holy life. Whatever Christ has promised to do He will do, and we must believe this so as to look for pardon, justification, preservation, and eternal glory from His hands.

Then comes the next necessary step. Jesus is what He is said to be and will do what He says He will do. Therefore we must *trust Him*, saying, "I leave myself in the hands of Him who is appointed to save, that He may save me. I rest upon His promise that He will do even as He has said." This is saving faith. What ever his dangers and difficulties, darkness and depression, weaknesses and sins, he who believes in Jesus Christ is not condemned.

Faith exists in various degrees according to the amount of knowledge or other causes. Sometimes faith is little more than a simple *clinging* to Christ in a sense of utter dependence. Thousands of God's people have no more faith than this. They know enough to cling to Jesus with all their heart and soul. Jesus Christ is to them a Savior strong and mighty, like an immovable and immutable rock. They cleave to Him for dear life, and this clinging saves them. God gives to His people the propensity to cling. Though this is a very simple sort of faith, it is a very complete and effectual form of it. In fact, it is the heart of all faith, and that to which we are often driven when we are in deep trouble or when our mind is somewhat bemuddled by sickness or depression in spirit. We can cling when we can do nothing else, and that is the very soul of faith. Always cling to what you know. If as yet you are only like a lamb that wades a little into the river of life and not like leviathan who stirs the mighty deep to the bottom, yet drink. For it is drinking and not diving that will save you. Cling to Jesus, for that is faith.

Another form of faith is when a man comes to depend upon another person from a recognition of superiority of that other and *follows* him. This next phase of faith involves more knowledge. A blind man trusts himself with his guide because he knows that his friend can see. The man born blind does not know what sight is, but he knows that there is such a thing as sight and that his friend possesses it. Therefore, he freely puts his hand into the hand of the seeing one and follows his leadership. This is as good an example of faith as can be given. We know that Jesus has in Himself the merit, power, and blessing that we do not possess. Therefore we gladly trust ourselves to Him, and He never betrays our confidence.

Every child who goes to school has to exert faith while *learning*. The teacher teaches him geography, instructing him as to the form of the earth and the existence of certain great cities and nations. The child does not know that these are true except that he believes his teacher and the book in his hands. That is what you will have to do with Christ if you are to be saved. You must simply know because He tells you and believe because He assures you it is so. Trust yourself with Him because He promises you that salvation will be the result. Almost all that you and I know has come to us by faith. A scientific discovery has been made, and we are sure of it. We believe on the authority of certain well-known scientists whose reputation is established. We have never made or seen the experiments, but we believe their witness. This is how we relate to Christ in faith. Because He teaches you certain truths, you are to be His disciple and believe His word and trust yourself to Him. He is infinitely superior to you and presents Himself to your confidence as your Master and Lord. If you will receive Him and His words, you will be saved.

Another and higher form of faith is faith that *grows out of love*. Why does a boy trust his father? You and I know a little more about his father than he does, and yet we do not rely upon him quite so implicitly. But the reason the child trusts his father is that he loves him. Blessed and happy are they who have a sweet faith in Jesus, intertwined with deep affection for Him. They are charmed with His character and delighted with His mission. They are carried away by the lovingkindness that He has manifested, and now they cannot help trusting Him because they so much admire, revere, and love Him. It is hard to make you doubt a person whom you love. If you are at last driven to doubt, then comes the awful passion of jealousy that is strong as death and cruel as the grave. But till such a crushing of the heart shall come, love is all trust and confidence.

The way of loving trust in the Savior may be shown in this illustration. The wife of the most eminent physician of the day is struck down with a dangerous illness, yet she is wonderfully calm and quiet. Her husband has made this disease his special study and has healed thousands similarly afflicted. She is not troubled, for she feels perfectly safe in the hands of one so dear to her, in whom skill and love are blended in their highest forms. Her faith is reasonable and natural, for her husband deserves it from every point of view. This is the kind of faith that the happiest believers exercise toward Christ. There is no physician like Him; none can save as He can. We love Him, and He loves us. Therefore we put ourselves in His hands, accepting whatever He prescribes and doing whatever He commands. We feel that nothing can be wrongly ordered while He is the director of our affairs, for He loves us too much to let us perish or suffer a single needless pang.

Faith also *realizes* the presence of the living God and Savior, breathing into the soul a beautiful calm and quiet like that seen in a little child during a thunderstorm. The child's mother was alarmed, but the sweet girl was pleased and clapped her hands with delight. Standing at the window when the flashes came most vividly, she cried, "Look, Mama! How beautiful! How beautiful!" Her mother said, "My dear, come away, the lightning is terrible." But the daughter begged to be allowed to look out and see the lovely light that God was making all over the sky, for she was sure God would not do His little child any harm. The little girl was as merry as a bird, for God was real to her and she trusted Him. To her the lightning was God's beautiful light and the thunder was God's wonderful voice, and she was happy. And though her mother knew a good deal about the laws of nature and the energy of electricity, her knowledge brought her little comfort. The child's knowledge was less showy, but it was far more certain and precious.

I would rather be a child again than to grow perversely wise. Faith is to be a child toward Christ, believing in Him as a real and present person who at this very moment is near us and ready to bless us. This may seem childish, but it is such a childishness as we must all come to if we would be happy in the Lord. "Except ye be converted, and become as little children, ye shall not enter into the kingdom of heaven" (Matt. 18:3). Faith takes Christ at His word, as a child believes his father, and trusts Him in all simplicity with the past, present, and future. God give us such faith!

A firm form of faith *arises out of assured knowledge*. This comes of growth in grace and is the faith that believes Christ because it knows Him, trusts Him because it has proved Him to be infallibly faithful. This faith does not ask for signs and wonders but bravely believes. I look with wonder upon the master mariner. How does he dare leave the safety of his port and find his way over the trackless deep? He trusts his compass, his nautical almanac, and the heavenly bodies, and obeys their guidance without sighting shore. To sail without sight is a wonderful thing. Spiritually it is a blessed thing to leave the shores of sight and say, "Goodbye to inward feelings, cheering providences, signs, wonders, and so forth. I believe in God, and I steer for heaven straight away." "Blessed are they that have not seen, and yet have believed" (John 20:29).

This is the faith that makes it easy *to commit our soul and all its eternal interests into the Savior's keeping.* One man goes to the bank and puts his money into it with a measure of confidence. Another man has looked into the bank's accounts and made sure of its having a large reserve of well-invested capital. That man puts in his money with utmost assurance. He knows and is established in his faith. Even so, we who know Christ are glad to place our whole being in His hands, knowing that He is able to keep us even unto the end.

May God give us more and more of an assured confidence in Jesus until it comes to be an unwavering faith that unquestionably believes. Look at the farmer who labors with his plow in the wintry months when there is not a bough on the tree or a bird that sings to cheer him. After he has plowed, he takes the seed corn and buries it in the furrows, assured that it will come up again. Because he has seen a harvest fifty times already, he looks for another and in faith scatters the precious seed. To all outward appearances, the most absurd thing is to bury the expensive seed in the ground. If you had never seen or heard of its results, it would seem a pure waste. Yet the farmer has no doubt and longs to plant his seed. If you tell him that he is doing an absurd thing, he smiles at your ignorance and tells you that this is the way to a harvest. Faith also grows by experience. Faith helps us to act in a manner contrary to all appearances. It leads us to commit our all to the keeping of Christ, burying our hopes and our very lives with Him in joyful confidence that if we are dead with Him we shall also live with Him. Jesus Christ who rose from the dead will raise us up through His death to newness of life and give us an eternal harvest of joy and peace.

May we get a strong faith so that we may never doubt the Savior's working for us in every hour of need. We have already trusted in our Lord and have never been confounded; therefore, let us go on to rely upon Him more and more implicitly. Never shall our faith in Him surpass the bounds of His deservings. Have faith in God, and then hear Jesus say, "Ye believe in God, believe also in me" (John 14:1).

Why Faith Is the Channel of Salvation

Why is faith selected as the channel of salvation? "For by grace are ye saved *through faith.*" It appears to me that faith has been selected as the channel of grace because *there is a natural adaptation* in faith to be used as the receiver. Faith is created on purpose to be a spiritual receiver. The faith that receives Christ is as simple an act as your child receiving an apple from you because you hold it out and promise to give the apple if the child comes for it. The belief and the receiving relate only to an apple, but they make up precisely the same act as the faith that deals with eternal salvation, and what the child's hand is to the apple, your faith is to the perfect salvation of Christ. The child's hand does not make or alter the apple; it only takes it. Faith is chosen by God to be the receiver of salvation because it does not pretend to make or help salvation, but it receives it.

Faith is doubtless selected because *it gives all the glory to God.* It is of faith that it might be by grace, and it is of grace that there may be no boasting, for God cannot endure pride. Paul adds, "Not of works, lest any man should boast" (Eph. 2:9). The hand that receives charity does not say to the body, "Thank me, for I feed you." It is a very simple thing that the hand does, though a very necessary thing, but it never arrogates glory to itself for what it does. God has selected faith to receive the unspeakable gift of His grace because it adores the gracious God who is the giver of all good.

God also selects faith as the channel of salvation because *it is a sure method, linking man with God.* When man confides in God, there is a point of union between them that guarantees blessing. Faith saves us because it makes us cling to God. I am told that years ago a boat was upset above the Niagara Falls, and two men were being carried down the current. Persons on the shore managed to float a rope out to them that was seized by them both. One of them held fast to it and was safely drawn to shore, but the other, seeing a great log floating by, unwisely let go of rope and grabbed the log. Apparently the log seemed more trustworthy because of its size. Alas, the log with the man on it went right over the vast abyss. So when a person trusts his works or sacraments or anything of that sort, there is no connection between him and Christ. But faith, though it may seem like a slender cord, is in the hand of the great God on the shore. Infinite power pulls in the connecting line and draws the person from destruction. Oh, the blessedness of faith, because it unites us to God!

Faith is chosen because *it touches the springs of action.* It seems to me that we never do anything except through faith of some sort. Whether we get up to walk or put food to our mouth, faith is involved. Columbus discovered America because he believed there was another continent beyond the ocean. Many grand deeds have also been born of faith, for faith works wonders. Faith in its natural form is an all-prevailing force. God gives salvation to our faith because He has thus touched the secret spring of all our emotions and actions. He has taken possession of the inner battery and can send the sacred current of His life to every part of our nature. When we believe in Christ and the heart has become the possession of God, we are saved from sin and move toward repentance, holiness, zeal, prayer, consecration, and every other gracious thing.

In particular, faith *has the power of working by love.* Faith touches the secret spring of the affections and draws the heart toward God. Faith is an act of understanding, but it proceeds to the heart. "For with the heart man believeth unto righteousness" (Rom. 10:10). God gives salvation to faith because it resides next door to the affections and is near to love, and love is that which purifies the soul. Love to God is obedience and holiness. To love God and to love man is to be conformed to the image of Christ, and this is salvation.

Moreover, *faith creates peace and joy.* He that has faith rests and is tranquil and joyous. God gives all the heavenly gifts to faith, because faith works in us the very life and spirit that is to be eternally manifested in heaven.

How Can Faith Be Obtained?

There are those who say they want to believe but cannot. Let us be practical in our dealing with it. The shortest way is to believe, and if the Holy Spirit has made you honest and candid, you will believe as soon as the truth is set before you. The gospel command is clear: "Believe on the Lord Jesus Christ, and thou shalt be saved" (Acts 16:31).

But still, *if you have difficulty, take it before God in prayer.* Tell the great Father exactly what it is that puzzles you and ask Him by His Holy Spirit to solve the question. If I cannot understand a statement in a book, I am glad to inquire of the author as to his meaning. The Lord is willing to make Himself known. Go to Him and see if it is not so.

Furthermore, if faith seems difficult, it is possible that God will enable you to believe if you *hear very frequently and sincerely that which you are commanded to believe.* We believe many things because we have heard them so often. If you hear a thing fifty times a day, at last you come to believe it. God often blesses this method in working faith concerning what is true, for it is written, "Faith cometh by hearing" (Rom. 10:17). If I sincerely and attentively hear the gospel, it may be that I shall find myself believing that which I hear.

I would add that you should *consider the testimony of others.* The Samaritans believed because of what the woman told them about Jesus (John 4:39). Many of our beliefs arise out of the testimony of others. I have never been to Japan, but I believe there is such a place because others have been there. I have never died, but I believe I shall die based on what I have seen through others' dying. Listen to those who tell you how they were saved and changed in character. If you listen, you will find that somebody just like yourself has been saved. If you have been a thief, you will find that a thief rejoiced to wash away his sin in the fountain of Christ's blood. You may have been unchaste in life, but you will find others who have been cleansed and changed. If you are in despair, you have only to get among God's people to find others who have been saved from despair. If you listen to another person who has tried the Word of God and proven it, the divine Spirit will lead you to believe. When you see others believe and notice their joy and peace, you will be gently led to believe. It is one of God's ways of helping us to faith.

A better method is to *note the authority upon which you are commanded to believe.* You are commanded to believe upon the authority of God Himself. *He* bids you believe in Jesus Christ, and you must not refuse to obey your Maker. We have His gracious invitation: "Come unto me, all ye that labor and are heavy laden, and I will give you rest" (Matt. 11:28). You cannot go wrong in coming to Him.

If that does not settle you, *think over what it is that you have to believe.* The good news is that the Lord Jesus Christ suffered in our place and is able to save all who trust Him. This is the most comforting, the most divine truth that ever was set before men. Consider it deeply and search out the grace and love that it contains. I bid you to *think upon the person of Jesus Christ*—think of who He is and what He did and where He is now and what He is now. Think often and deeply. Study the four gospels, study Paul's epistles, and then see if the message is not such a credible one that you are forced to believe it.

My last word is to *submit yourself to God.* May the Spirit of God help you to yield to His grace. Give up your rebellion; throw down your weapons; yield at discretion; surrender to your King. I believe that when a soul cries out, "Lord, I yield to You," faith becomes an easy thing. But if you still have a quarrel with God and intend to have your own will and way, you will not be able to believe. Proud self creates unbelief. Yield to your God, and then shall you sweetly believe in your Savior.

Do you propose to bribe God with your money? Surely you are not so foolish. The Lord could not be bought with a row of cathedrals. The silver and gold are His, and the cattle on a thousand hills. If He were hungry, He would not tell you. What can you give to Him to whom all things belong? Whatever you bring is a trifle as to cause any delight in God. Solomon built Him a marvelous temple, but "the Most High dwelleth not in temples made with hands" (Acts 7:48). The most glorious cathedral can at best be likened to the anthills of the tropics that are the wonderful fabrication of ants. What are anthills or cathedrals when measured with the Infinite? What are all the works of the Lord? He who with a single arch has spanned the world cares little for our carved capitals and lovely arches. "Will the LORD be pleased with thousands of rams, or with ten thousands of rivers of oil? shall I give my firstborn for my transgression, the fruit of my body for the sin of my soul?" (Mic. 6:7). It is not this that He asks of you but to walk humbly with Him, never daring arrogantly to doubt His truth and mistrust His faithfulness. Do not dash your ship upon this iron-bound coast of a lack of faith. Believe in your God.

Chapter Three

Faith Essential to Pleasing God

But without faith it is impossible to please him: for he that cometh to God must believe that he is, and that he is a rewarder of them that diligently seek him—Heb. 11:6.

PEOPLE HAVE LIVED who have pleased God. Enoch was one such person, but he was not the only one (Heb. 11:5). In all ages certain persons have been well pleasing to God, and their walk in life has been such as was His delight. It should be the aim of everyone to please God, and it is possible, despite our imperfections and weaknesses. Let us aim at pleasing God in the power of the Holy Spirit. What has been wrought in one person may be wrought in another. If we so live as to please the Lord, we shall only be acting as we should act. He is our God and Lord, and obedience is the highest law of our being. Moreover, the glorious Jehovah is so perfectly good, so supremely holy, that the conduct that pleases Him must be of the best and noblest sort. Should we not aspire to that character upon which God Himself can smile? The approval of others is pleasant in its way, but others are always imperfect and often mistaken. It is possible to be pleasing to them and yet remain far from righteousness. But God makes no mistake. The Infinitely Holy knows no imperfection. If it is possible for us to be pleasing to Him, it should be our one object to do so. As Enoch was pleasing to Him in a darker age, why should we not be upon whom the gospel day has dawned? God grant us to find grace in His sight!

If we please God, we shall have realized the reason for our being. It is written concerning all things: "for thou hast created all things, and for thy pleasure they are and were created" (Rev. 4:11). We miss the end of creation if we are not pleasing to the Lord. To fulfill God's end in our creation is to obtain the highest joy. If we are pleasing to God, although we shall not escape trial, for even the highest qualities must be tested, we shall find great peace and special happiness. He is not an unhappy man who pleases God. God has blessed him, and he shall be blessed. By pleasing God we shall become the means of good to others. Our example will rebuke and stimulate; our peace will convince and invite. The godly man will teach transgressors God's way, and sinners shall come to Christ. I urge you then to win this testimony of being pleasing to God.

The writer of Hebrews brings us practical instructions on this. *He asserts that faith is absolutely needful if we would please God.* Then, to help us further, *he mentions two essential points of faith:* "he that cometh to God must believe that he is, and that he is a rewarder of them that diligently seek him." I would like to explore these closer.

The Essential Nature of Faith

Take the key word from our verse: "Without faith it is *impossible* to please God." He does not say it is difficult or nearly possible, but pointblank he declares it is *impossible*. When the Holy Spirit records that a thing is impossible, it is so in a very absolute sense. Let us not attempt the impossible. To attempt a difficulty may be commendable, but to rush upon an impossibility is madness. We must not hope to please God by any invention of our own, however clever, or by any labor of our own, however ardent. Infallible inspiration declares that "without faith it is impossible to please God."

There are many reasons why this is so. *Without faith there is no capacity for communion with God at all.* The things of God are spiritual and invisible. Without faith we cannot see such things but are dead to them. Faith is the eye that sees, and without that eye we are blind. We can have no fellowship with God in the sacred truths that only faith can perceive. Faith is the hand of the soul, and without it we cannot grasp eternal things. It is only by faith that we can recognize God, approach Him, speak to Him, hear Him, feel His presence, and be delighted with His perfections. Where there is no faith, there has been no quickening of the Holy Spirit, for faith is of the very essence of spiritual life. He who has not faith is dead toward God, and Jehovah is the God not of the dead but of the living.

Without faith the man himself is not pleasing to God. Perhaps the Revised text has it better: "Without faith it is impossible to be well-pleasing unto God." The way of acceptance described in Scripture is that the man is first accepted, and then what that man does is accepted. It is written: "he shall purify the sons of Levi . . . that they may offer unto the LORD an offering in righteousness" (Mal. 3:3). God is pleased first with the person and then with the gift or work. The unaccepted person offers an unacceptable sacrifice. If a person is your enemy, you will not value a present that he sends you. If you know a person praises you only for personal gain, you recognize the praises as empty, deceptive things that cannot possibly bring you pleasure.

God cannot look upon us as sinners with complacency. Concerning our race it is written: "it repented the LORD that he had made man on the earth, and it grieved him at his heart" (Gen. 6:6). Is this true of us? Jesus said, "Except a man be born again, he cannot see the kingdom of God" (John 3:3). It is only to as many as receive Him that He gives power to become the sons of God. When we believe in the Lord Jesus, God accepts us for His beloved's sake. In Christ we are made kings and priests and permitted to bring an offering that pleases God. As the man is, such is his work. The stream is of the nature of the spring from which it flows. He who is a rebel cannot gratify his prince by any manner of service until he submits to the law. All the actions of rebels are acts done in rebellion. We must first be reconciled to God, or it is a mockery to bring an offering to His altar. Faith in Christ makes a total change in our position toward God. We who were enemies are reconciled, and from this comes toward God a distinct change in the nature of all our actions. Though our actions may be imperfect, they spring from a loyal heart and are pleasing to God.

Remember that in human relationships *lack of confidence can prevent a man's being well pleasing to another.* If you have a child who does not trust you, does not believe your kindness, and cannot rely upon your word, it is most painful for you as a parent and impossible that you should take any pleasure in such a child. If someone who works for you always suspects your every action, does not believe anything that you say, and questions all your motives, it makes for an impossible working relationship. A lack of confidence destroys any pleasure that one might have in another. When a person dares to doubt his Creator, how can the Creator be pleased? When the word that wrought creation is not enough for a man to rest upon, that man may pretend what he will of righteousness and obedience, but the whole affair is rotten at the core. God can take no pleasure in it.

Unbelief takes away the common ground upon which God and man can meet. Since God's great object is the glorification of His Son, how can we be pleasing to Him if we dishonor that Son? The Father delights in Jesus: "This is my beloved Son, in whom I am well pleased" (Matt. 3:17). The Father later added for others to heed: "This is my beloved Son: hear him" (Luke 9:35). He delights in what His Son has done and is pleased with His atoning sacrifice. If you and I believe in God's plan of salvation through Jesus Christ, we have a common ground of sympathy with God. But if not, we are not in harmony. If Jesus is despised, rejected, distrusted, or even neglected, it is not possible for us to be pleasing to God. If you will not even trust Jesus with your soul's salvation, you grieve the heart of God, and He can have no pleasure in you. Unbelief deprives the soul of the divinely appointed meeting place at the mercy seat, which is the person of Jesus Christ, where God and man unite in one Mediator.

Assuredly, *a lack of faith destroys all prospect of love.* Although we may not perhaps see it, there lies at the bottom of all love a belief in the object loved as to its loveliness, merit, and capacity to make us happy. If I do not believe in a person, I cannot love him. If I cannot trust God, I cannot love Him. If I do not believe that He loves me, how shall I feel love to Him? If I refuse to see anything in the greatest display of His love, if I do not value the gift of His dear Son, I cannot love Him. "We love him, because he first loved us" (1 John 4:19). If we reject His love, we have put away from our heart the grand incentive to love. But love on our part is essential to our pleasing God. Is not the Lord's chief demand of men that we love Him with all our heart, soul, mind, and strength? Without faith, love is impossible, and God's pleasure in us must be impossible.

A lack of faith will create disagreements at many points. If I trust God, I shall submit my will even when it becomes very painful. We will say, "It is the LORD: let him do what seemeth him good" (1 Sam. 3:18). But if I do not believe that He is aiming at my good, I shall resent His disciplines and kick against His will. What He allows me to suffer, I shall not be willing to suffer. But I shall rebel, murmur, and proudly accuse my Maker of injustice or lack of love. "The LORD taketh pleasure in them that fear him, in those that hope in his mercy" (Ps. 147:11). But He will walk contrary to us if we walk contrary to Him.

Without faith we find ourselves in disagreement with God about salvation. Inasmuch as I desire to be saved, I shall seek salvation in my own way and try to establish a righteousness of my own. Whatever it may be, whether by ceremonies or good works or feelings, I shall set up a way of salvation other than that which God has appointed through Christ Jesus. But God will not endure that a rival should be set up in opposition to His way. Self-righteousness is an insult to Christ and a distinct revolt from God. Such a derogatory way cannot please God.

"He that believeth not God hath made him a liar; because he believeth not the record that God gave of his Son" (1 John 5:10). This is the crime of the unbeliever. Could you take any pleasure in a person who made you out to be a liar? Perhaps with great patience you could bear with him, but you could not be pleased with him. By his actions and words he makes you something you are not. Nothing he could do would please you while he calls you a liar. He that makes God to be a liar makes Him to be no God. To the best of his ability the unbeliever undeifies the Deity and uncrowns the Lord of all, even stabbing at the heart of the Eternal. To talk of being well pleasing to God in such a case is absurd.

Let me ask *by what means we can hope to please God apart from faith*? By keeping all the commandments? Alas! You have not done so. You have already broken them and continue to do so in a chronic state of disobedience. True obedience commands the understanding as well as every other power and faculty. We are bound to obey with the mind by believing. The spiritual part of our being is in revolt against God until we believe.

Do you propose to bribe God with your money? Surely you are not so foolish. The Lord could not be bought with a row of cathedrals. The silver and gold are His, and the cattle on a thousand hills. If He were hungry, He would not tell you. What can you give to Him to whom all things belong? Whatever you bring is a trifle as to cause any delight in God. Solomon built Him a marvelous temple, but "the Most High dwelleth not in temples made with hands" (Acts 7:48). The most glorious cathedral can at best be likened to the anthills of the tropics that are the wonderful fabrication of ants. What are anthills or cathedrals when measured with the Infinite? What are all the works of the Lord? He who with a single arch has spanned the world cares little for our carved capitals and lovely arches. "Will the LORD be pleased with thousands of rams, or with ten thousands of rivers of oil? shall I give my firstborn for my transgression, the fruit of my body for the sin of my soul?" (Mic. 6:7). It is not this that He asks of you but to walk humbly with Him, never daring arrogantly to doubt His truth and mistrust His faithfulness. Do not dash your ship upon this iron-bound coast of a lack of faith. Believe in your God.

Two Essential Points of Faith

The writer of Hebrews begins by saying, "He that cometh to God *must* believe that He is." The key word is *must*—an immovable, insatiable necessity. Before we can walk with God, it is clear that we must *come to God*. The distance between Him and us must be ended by our coming to Him. And to come to Him, we must believe there is a God. Only a fool doubts that: "The fool hath said in his heart, There is no God" (Ps. 53:1). But we must believe that Jehovah is God, and God alone. You must accept Jehovah as He reveals Himself. You are not to have a God of your own making or a God reasoned out but a God such as He has been pleased to reveal Himself to you.

The devils believe and tremble, and yet they are not pleasing to God (James 2:19). Many believe that there is a hazy, imaginary power who they call God, but they never think of Him as a person or suspect that He thinks of them. Believe that God *is* as truly real as you are. Let the consideration of Him enter into everything that concerns you. Believe that He is approachable by yourself and is pleased or displeased by you. Believe in God beyond everything, that "He is" in a sense more sure than anything or anyone.

Hold this as the primary truth that God is more influential upon you. Then believe that it is your business to come to Him. But there is only one way of coming to Him: "Jesus said unto him, I am the way, the truth, and the life: no man cometh unto the Father, but by me" (John 14:6). Faith comes to God as God reveals the way of approach. If you can live from Monday morning to Saturday night in the same way as you would live if there were no God, you are a practical atheist despite your church involvement. Actions speak more loudly than words, and a life without God is as bad as a creed without God.

Yet all this would be nothing without the second point of belief. We must believe that "he is a rewarder of them that diligently seek him." How do we *seek Him*? We seek Him when we begin by prayer, by trusting in Jesus, and by calling upon the sacred name. "Whoever shall call on the name of the Lord shall be saved" (Acts 2:21). That is a grand promise, and it teaches how we come to God. Afterward we seek God by aiming at His glory, by making Him the great object for which we live. One man seeks money, another seeks reputation, another seeks pleasure, but he who pleases God seeks God as his object and end. "But seek ye first the kingdom of God, and his righteousness; and all these things shall be added unto you" (Matt. 6:33). The person with whom God is pleased is pleased with God. He sets the Lord always before him and seeks to live for Him. And this is done on the basis that God will reward him in doing so. We are sure that somehow or other it will be to our highest benefit to honor the Lord and trust in Him. While we deserve nothing at His hands but wrath, yet we perceive in the gospel that if we seek Him through His Son, we shall be so well pleasing to Him as to get a reward from His hands. This must be of free, sovereign grace. And what a reward it is! Free pardon, graciously bestowed; a change of heart, graciously wrought; perseverance, graciously maintained; comfort, graciously poured in; and privilege, graciously awarded. The reward of godliness, even in this world, is immeasurable, and in the world to come it is infinite!

"A rewarder of them that diligently seek him" is not an exact translation. The Greek word means not only to seek Him but "seek Him out"; that is, seek Him till they find Him and seek Him above all others. It is a very strong word. We must seek and seek out until we really find. Those who with their hearts follow after God shall not be losers if they believe that He will reward them. Even when you do not obtain any present reward, you may say, "I shall have a reward ultimately, even if I am for a while a loser through His service. I may lose money, respect, friendship, or even my life, yet still He will be a rewarder and I shall be repaid a thousandfold according to His grace."

Be certain that to serve God is in itself gain. It is wealth to be holy. It is happiness to be pleasing to God. To us it is life to live to God—to know Him, to adore Him, to commune with Him, to become like Him. It is glory for us to make Him glorious among the sons of men. God is our shield and our exceeding great reward. We cannot conceive that the heavenly Father looks with displeasure upon a man struggling against sin, battling evil, enduring sorrow contentedly through a simple faith, and laboring daily to draw nearer and nearer to Him. God is pleased with those who by faith live to please Him and are content to take their reward from His hand. He must be pleased with the work of His own grace. The desire to come to God, the way to come, the power to come, and the actual coming to God are all gifts of sovereign grace. Coming to God, however feeble and however much else we miss, must be well pleasing in His sight. For it is the result of His own purpose and grace that He gave us in Christ Jesus before the world began.

Practical Lessons About Our Faith

We discover that *God is pleased with those who have faith.* If we are so carefully warned that without faith it is impossible to please God, we infer that with faith it is possible to please God. By faith we ourselves have become pleasing to God, and our actions performed with a view to His honor are pleasing to Him. What a joy is this! It is bliss to think that I who have grieved and vexed the

Holy Spirit am now the object of pleasure to Him. I, who lived contrary to the law of God and the gospel of Christ, I, even I, who was once obnoxious to Divine anger and an heir of wrath, have now become to God an object of His pleasure through faith. This is very wonderful. If the Holy Spirit leads you to feel the full sweetness of this truth, you will rejoice with joy unspeakable. It sets my soul to singing. If faith can make the vilest and guiltiest pleasing to God, will you not believe in Him? What a transformation this works!

We learn that *those who have faith make it the great object of their lives to please God*. The believer in the invisible God delights to act as in His sight and in secret to serve Him. I take pleasure in rendering to my God a service unknown to others, not done for the sake of others, but distinctly that I may do something for my Lord. It is sweet to give or do simply to please *Him* without respect to the public eye. Even such actions as must come under the gaze of others are not to be done with the view of winning their approbation but only to please God. The doing of such is a singular fountain of strength to a man's mind. It is ennobling to feel you have only one Master and that you live to *please Him*. To please men is poor work. To live to follow everybody's whim is slavery. If you let one man pull you by the ear in his direction, another will tug at you from another direction, and you will have very long ears before long.

To live to please God gives a man backbone and at the same time removes the selfishness that is greedy for popular applause. It is a grand thing to no longer look down for cheer but to distinctly look up for it. The man who truly believes in God makes small account of men. To please God even a little is infinitely greater than to have the acclamations of all our race throughout the centuries. The true believer feels that God is and that there is none beside Him, none that needs to be thought of in comparison with Him. And only as we see men loved of God can we live for men, seeking their good in God and for His glory and regarding them as capable of being made mirrors to reflect the glory of the Lord.

The epistle writer also teaches us that *they that have faith in God are always coming to Him*, for he speaks of the believer as "he that cometh to God." You not only come to Him in acts of prayer and praise, but you are always coming. Your life becomes a march toward Him. By his faith the believer comes ever nearer and yet nearer to the eternal throne. What is the reward? Why, He that sits on the throne will say, "Come, ye blessed of my Father, inherit the kingdom prepared for you from the foundation of the world" (Matt. 25:34). Come! Come on! You have been coming; keep on coming forever. There is a gentle, constant, perpetual progress of the believer's heart and mind nearer and closer to God. I could not wonder at Enoch's being translated after walking with God hundreds of years, for it is such a small step from close communion with God on earth to perfect communion with God in heaven. A thin partition divides us which a sigh will remove. The breaking of a blood vessel, the loss of breath, the snapping of a cord, and he who had God with him shall be with God. Live to please God, and as you please Him by your simple confidence and childlike trust, you are coming nearer to Him.

Another lesson is that *God will see that those who practice faith in Him shall have a reward.* I say that God will see to it because the text reads: "He is a rewarder." The Lord will not leave the reward of faith to the choicest angels but will do it Himself. Seldom on earth are we rewarded fairly from those we benefit. We often only receive base ingratitude. Expect little from men and much from God, for by nature and office He is a rewarder. No work done for Him will go unrewarded. In His service the wages are sure. Rise into the Abrahamic life that stays itself upon the Lord's word: "Fear not, Abram: I am thy shield, and thy exceeding great reward" (Gen. 15:1). It is enough to have such a God to be our God. What if He gives us nothing besides Himself? Surely this is greater rewarder than if He gave us all the world. A faith true and deep cries, "Whom have I in heaven but thee? and there is none upon earth that I desire beside thee" (Ps. 73:25).

The last lesson we gather is that *those who have no faith are in a fearful state.* "Without faith it is impossible to please God." I know people who seem to be always shaping fresh nets of doubt to get entangled in. Like mariners who seek the rocks or soldiers who court the point of a bayonet, this is unprofitable business. Practically, morally, mentally, and spiritually, doubting is an evil trade. Doubt is sterile, a desert without water. Doubt discovers difficulties that it never solves and creates hesitancy, despondency, despair. Its progress is the decay of comfort, the death of peace. *Believe* is the word that speaks life into a man, but doubt nails down his coffin. I entreat you to look up and see the pierced hands and feet and side of the dear Redeemer. Read eternal mercy and full forgiveness there, and then go your way in peace, for you are well pleasing to God. He will receive you graciously and love you freely. Come to Him for He is a rewarder of them that diligently seek Him.

*W*hen our personal biographies are written someday, God grant that they may not be all sayings but that they may be a history of our sayings and our doings! May the good Spirit so dwell in us that at the end of our lives it may be seen that our doings do not clash with our sayings! It is one thing to preach but another thing to practice, and unless our preaching and practice go together, the preacher is himself condemned. If you make a profession of being God's servant, live up to that profession. If you think it is necessary to exhort others to virtue, take care that you set the example. You can have no right to teach others if you have not learned the lesson yourself.

Chapter Four

Characteristics of Faith

Then said Jesus unto him, Except ye see signs and wonders, ye will not believe—John 4:48.

WHEN LUKE WROTE HIS LETTER to Theophilus, he spoke of things that Jesus "began both to do and teach" (Acts 1:1), indicating there was a connection between Jesus' doings and teachings. In fact, there *was* a relation of the most intimate kind. Jesus' teachings were the explanation of His doings, and His doings were a confirmation of His teachings. Jesus Christ never had the occasion to say, "Do as I say but not as I do." His words and actions were in perfect harmony with one another. You may be sure that Jesus was honest in what He *said*, because what He *did* forced that conviction upon your mind. Moreover, you were led to see that what Jesus taught you must be true because He spoke with a marvelous authority that was proven and demonstrated by the miracles He worked.

When our personal biographies are written someday, God grant that they may not be all sayings but that they may be a history of our sayings *and* our doings! May the good Spirit so dwell in us that at the end of our lives it may be seen that our doings do not clash with our sayings! It is one thing to preach but another thing to practice, and unless our preaching and practice go together, the preacher is himself condemned. If you make a profession of being God's servant, live up to that profession. If you think it is necessary to exhort others to virtue, take care that you set the example. You can have no right to teach others if you have not learned the lesson yourself.

How important, then, it becomes to understand our Christian faith and how it works in our lives! With John 4:46–54 as a background, I hope to draw out three essential matters that Jesus makes concerning faith.

Three Stages of Faith

There is a nobleman living in Capernaum who has heard a rumor that a celebrated prophet and preacher is continually going through the cities of Galilee and Judea. The nobleman understands that this mighty preacher does not merely enthrall every listener by His eloquence but wins the hearts of men by benevolent miracles that He works as a confirmation of His mission. The day comes when the nobleman's son—perhaps his only son, one very dear to his father's heart—falls sick. Instead of diminishing, the illness gradually increases. Fever breathes its hot breath upon the child and seems to dry up all the moisture of his body and blasts the bloom from his cheeks. The father consults every physician within his reach, but they candidly pronounce the child hopeless. No cure can possibly be worked. The nobleman's son is at the point of death; the arrow of death has almost sunk into his flesh and will soon penetrate his heart. Death's very point has been forced upon the child by the barbed arrows of that insatiate archer.

The nobleman recalls the stories he has heard of the cures wrought by a man named Jesus of Nazareth. Though there is little faith in his soul, he determines to make every attempt to test the truth of the stories that he has heard. Jesus Christ has come to Cana again and is only fifteen or twenty miles away. Travelling with all speed and with hope building in his soul, the nobleman arrives at the place where Jesus is. Seeing the Master, he begins to cry, "Lord, come down before my child dies!" But the Master, instead of giving an answer that might console the desperate father, rebukes the nobleman for the littleness of his faith, telling him, "Except ye see signs and wonders, ye will not believe." The man, however, pays little attention to the rebuke, for there is a desire that has absorbed all the powers of his soul. His mind is so overwhelmed with one anxiety that he is oblivious to anything else. "Sir," said he, "come down ere my child die." The nobleman has arrived at the *first state of faith* where he pleads in prayer, earnestly imploring the Lord to come and heal his son. The Master looks upon him with an eye of ineffable kindness and says, "Go thy way; thy son liveth."

Trusting in Jesus' word without a shred of evidence as confirmation, the father went his way quickly, contentedly, and cheerfully. He has come to the *second stage of his faith* where he no longer is seeking but is relying. He does not plead anymore that the healing will be given, even though he has not seen the gift given yet. It is not until he is on the road home that his servants meet him with the joyful news: "Thy son liveth." Enquiring at what time the fever left his son, the nobleman discovers that it was the exact time when Jesus said, "Thy son liveth."

Then the nobleman comes to the *third stage of faith*. He goes home and sees his child perfectly restored. The child springs in his arms, covering him with kisses. After holding the child up again and again to make sure that he is really well, the nobleman triumphs in a higher sense. His faith moves beyond reliance up to full assurance, and then his whole house believed as well as himself.

Having outlined the three stages of faith from the biblical narrative, I would like to examine each more closely:

Seeking Faith

When faith begins in the soul, it is but as a grain of mustard seed. God's people are not born giants but are born as babes, and as they are babes in grace, so their graces are as it were in their infancy. When God first gives faith to a person, it is not a fire but a spark—a spark that seems like it will go out but is nevertheless fanned and kept alive until it comes to flame, growing into the vehement heat of Nebuchadnezzar's furnace. The nobleman in the biblical narrative, when he had faith given to him, had only the smallest amount of faith. It was seeking faith. That is the first stage of faith. It was just enough faith to stimulate the nobleman to action.

A person with seeking faith is no longer indifferent or careless about the things of God. Seeking faith causes him to pay attention to the means of grace, leads him to search the Word of God and to be diligent in the use of every ordained means of blessing for the soul. If there is a sermon to be heard, seeking faith puts wings under the feet to get there. If there is a congregation experiencing revival, seeking faith makes one willing to stand through the service that he might hear the Word that has come with power. Seeking faith causes a person to lean forward that he may not lose a syllable, for, "Perhaps," he says, "the sentence that I lose may be the very one that I need." The seeker becomes among the most enthusiastic of hearers and the most earnest of those who attend that place of worship.

More than this, seeking faith, though it is very weak in some things, gives a person great power in prayer. How sincere was this nobleman: "Lord, come down ere my child die." When seeking faith enters into the soul, it makes a man pray. He is not content now with muttering over a few words when he rises in the morning and ringing the same chimes at night when he goes to bed. If he can, he takes a quarter hour of his day to cry to God in secret. He has not the faith yet to say, "My sins are forgiven," but he has faith enough to know that Christ *can* forgive his sins, and what he wants is that he may know that *his* sins are really forgiven. Sometimes this man has no access to a church to pray, but seeking faith will make him pray in the barn, in his room, in his place of business, or even walking the street. Satan may throw a thousand difficulties in the way, but seeking faith will compel the person to knock at mercy's door. Seeking faith has but to be nourished, to be cherished, to be exercised, and the little spark shall become mighty. Seeking faith shall come to a higher degree of development, and those who knock at mercy's gate shall enter in and find a place of welcome at Jesus' table.

Notice further in the nobleman's case that seeking faith did not simply make him earnest in prayer but made him persistent in pray. He asked once, and the only answer he received was an apparent rebuff. He did not turn away in a sulk. No. "Sir," he said, "come down ere my child die." I cannot tell you how he said it, but I have no doubt it was expressed in soul-moving terms, with tears starting from his eyes and hands placed together in the attitude of entreaty. He seemed to say, "I cannot let you go unless you come and save my child. Please, do come. Is there anything I can say that can get you to come? Let a father's affection be my best argument. If my lips are not eloquent, let the tears of my eyes supply the place of the words of my tongue."

What mighty prayers are those that seeking faith will make a person pray! I have heard the seeker sometimes plead with God with all the power that Jacob ever could have had at Jabbok's brook (Gen. 32:24–32). I have seen the sinner under distress of soul seem to take hold of the pillars of the gate of mercy and rock them to and fro as though he would sooner pull them up from their deep foundations than go away without effecting an entrance. I have seen sinners pull and tug, strive and fight and wrestle, rather than not enter the kingdom of heaven. No wonder that those who come before God with cold prayers do not find peace. Heat them red hot in the furnace of desire and they will burn their way upward to heaven. Those who merely say in the chill form of orthodoxy, "God be merciful to me a sinner," will never find mercy. It is the person who cries in the burning anguish of heartfelt emotion: "God be merciful to *me* a sinner! Save *me* or I perish!" who gains his plea. It is the person who concentrates his soul in every word and flings the violence of his being into every sentence that wins his way through the gates of heaven. Seeking faith can make a person do this.

There is a weakness to seeking faith. It can do much good, but it makes many mistakes. Seeking faith knows too little, for note that the nobleman said, "Sir, come down." Jesus did not need to come down. The Lord can work the miracle without going anywhere. But seeking faith could only see the Master literally touching his son. It often dictates to God how He will save the person. Some people desire that God send them some terrible convictions and then they think they can believe. Others seek a dream, a vision, a sign and wonder, or to hear a voice saying to them, "Your sins are forgiven." Seeking faith is strong enough to make a person pray, but it is not strong enough to cast out of the mind silly ideas. Like the nobleman, the seeker must allow God to have His sovereign way of bringing His blessing into his life. The nobleman must be willing to let Jesus speak the word and that be enough. So the seeker must not put before God certain requirements for His working.

Relying Faith

The Master stretched out His hand and said, "Go thy way; thy son liveth." Do you see the face of the nobleman? Those worried furrows engraved in his forehead seem to be smoothed in a moment and are gone. Those eyes are full of tears, but they are tears of joy. He claps his hands, retires silently, his heart ready to burst with gratitude, his whole soul full of confidence. "Why are you so happy, sir?" "Because my child is cured," he says. "But you have not seen him cured." "True. But my Lord said the child was, and I believe Jesus." "But what if your faith is a delusion and the child is a corpse." "It cannot be. I believe in that man. Once I believed Him and sought Him. Now I believe Him and have found Him. The naked word of that divine prophet is enough for me. He spoke it, and I know it is true. He told me to go my way for my son is alive. I go my way, and I am quite at peace."

When faith gets to a second stage where it takes Christ at His word, then a person begins to know the happiness of believing, and then it is that faith saves the soul. "Believe on the Lord Jesus Christ, and thou shalt be saved" (Acts 16:31). "But I feel no evidence." Believe it nonethless for that. "But," says another, "I do not feel enjoyment in my heart." Believe it, though your heart may have never felt so gloomy. Enjoyment shall come afterwards. It is a heroic faith that believes Christ in the face of a thousand contradictions. When the Lord gives you that faith, you can say, "I do not look to others. He who said to me, 'Believe and be saved,' gave me the grace to believe, and I therefore am confident that I am saved. Sink or swim, I have cast my soul upon the love and blood and power of Christ. Though there may be no witness to my soul, though doubts distress me and fears plague me, yet it is mine to honor my Master by believing His Word." Though others hiss and hoot and scorn, that person has become a disciple who says, "I believe my Master. What He has said I believe is true." When you, in the teeth of everything that is conflicting, stand to Christ and believe His words, you do Christ greater homage than cherubim and seraphim before the throne. Dare to believe. Trust Christ, and you are saved.

In this second stage of faith, the person begins to enjoy quietness and peace of mind. The fifteen to twenty miles between Cana and Capernaum would not have taken the nobleman long to travel home. Yet, it is evident from the text that it was the following day before the nobleman's servants met him on the way. I draw this inference that the nobleman was so sure that his child was alive and well that he was in no immediate hurry to return. It appears that given the seventh hour that Jesus spoke the word, the nobleman went his way leisurely and calmly, confident in the truth of what Jesus had said to him. He who takes the word of Christ to be the basis of his hope stands on a rock while other ground is sinking sand. Although Jesus may not take you into His banqueting houses, still trust Him. If you find yourself locked away in a dungeon, still trust Him. Afflictions may stick in your flesh and all may have gone wrong, but still trust Him. Say with Job, "Though he slay me, yet will I trust him." Your righteousness shall come forth as the light and your glory as a lamp that burns.

The Full Assurance of Faith

The servants meet the nobleman with the news that his son is healed. The man arrives at home, clasps his child and sees him perfectly restored. The nobleman's reaction was that of assured faith: "himself believed, and his whole house." And yet you will notice that in the fiftieth verse, it says that he believed: "And the man believed the word that Jesus had spoken unto him." This has been a puzzle for many expositors. When did the man believe? John Calvin comments that this man had in the first place only a faith that relied for one thing upon Christ. The man believed the word Christ had spoken. Afterward he had a faith that took Christ into his soul, making him a disciple who trusted Christ as the Messiah. This is an illustration of faith in its highest state. The nobleman found his son healed at the very hour when Jesus said he would be. "And now," the nobleman says, "I believe"; that is to say, he believed with full assurance of faith. His mind was so rid of its doubts that he believed in Jesus of Nazareth as the Christ of God.

I have known people who say, "If I had the full assurance of faith, then I could believe I am a child of God." The secret is to first believe Christ's naked word, and then you shall come afterwards to feel in your soul the witness of the Spirit that you are born of God. Assurance is a flower that must first be planted as a bulb. Plant the bulb of faith first, and you shall eventually have the flower. The shrivelled seed of a little faith springs upward, and then you have the ripe corn in the ear of full assurance of faith.

But notice that when the nobleman came to the full assurance of faith, it says that his house believed also. It is so similar to the verse concerning the jailor in Acts 16:31: "Believe on the Lord Jesus Christ, and thou shalt be saved, *and thy house*." Does the father's faith save the family? Yes! No!—*Yes*, it does in the sense that the father's faith makes him pray for his family, and God hears his prayer, and the family is saved. *No*, the father's faith cannot be a substitute for the faith of the children, for they must believe also. When a man has believed, there is a promise that his house will be saved. The father should not rest satisfied until he sees all his children saved. If he does rest, he has not believed correctly. Yet, there are those who only believe for themselves. Take the promise as broadly as the Word states and claim from God your little ones as well.

Three Illnesses of Faith

Seeking Faith

The power of seeking faith lies in it driving a person to prayer. And here is where the disease attacks. When we are seeking to begin, we are tempted to suspend prayerfulness. How often does the devil whisper in a man's ear, "Don't bother. Prayer is of no use. God will not listen to you." Or, when a person thinks he has received an answer to prayer, Satan says, "You need not pray any more. You have what you asked for." Or, if after a month of pleading with God and then receiving, Satan whispers, "See how reluctant your God was. There is no mercy at the gate. Be gone! The gate is finally nailed up, and you will never be heard again!" If you are subject to this illness while seeking Christ, I bid you cry against it and labor against it. Never cease to pray. A man can never sink in the river of wrath so long as he can cry. So long as you can cry to God for mercy, mercy shall never withdraw itself from you.

Never allow Satan to push you back from the door of prayer. Push the door in, whether Satan gives up or not. To give up prayer is to seal your own damnation. Renounce the place of supplication, and you renounce Christ and heaven. Continue in prayer, and though the answer may be delayed, it must come. In God's time, He will answer you.

Relying Faith

The disease that most likely falls upon those who trust Christ implicitly is the illness of wanting to see signs and wonders as a condition for faith. Were I to tell you the whims and fancies that some people get into their heads, you might smile or you might weep. People patch up almost any strange fancy to make themselves think that they may then trust Christ. If you have no better reason to believe you are in Christ than a dream or a vision, it is time you begin again. It is true that some become alarmed, convinced, and perhaps converted by strange freaks of their imagination. But if you rely on these as being pledges from God, if you look on these as being evidences that you are saved, you are resting on a dream and delusion. You may as well seek to build a castle in the air.

He who believes Christ, believes Christ because Christ is worthy of trust and because it is written in the Word. He does not believe it because he dreamed it or a heard a strange voice or thought he saw an angel. If a sign or wonder comes, be thankful. If they do not come, trust simply in the Word of God. To put your reliance on a sign or wonder is to open the door to being deceived. The Bible is the sure word of testimony that you do well to take heed to as a light that shines in a dark place. Trust in the Lord and wait patiently for Him. Cast all your confidence on the One who put all your sins upon Christ Jesus alone—with or without any of these signs and wonders.

There are Christians in London who have been meeting in special prayer gatherings to seek revival. But because people have not been dropping down in a fainting spell or screaming and making noise, they have thought the revival has not come. Oh, that we might have eyes to see God's gifts in the way God chooses to give them! We do not need the revival that occurred in northern Ireland. We need a true revival, but not in that particular shape. If the Lord sends it in another form, we should be as happy even if it has no outward displays. Where the Spirit works in the soul, we are always glad to see true conversion, and if He chooses to work in outward manifestations, too, we will be glad. If men's hearts are renewed, what does it matter if they do not scream it out? If their consciences are made alive, does it matter whether they collapse motionless and senseless? Take it without signs and wonders. I have no personal craving for signs and wonders. But let me see God's work done in God's way—a true and thorough revival.

The Full Assurance of Faith

The disease that attacks our attaining a full assurance of faith is the lack of observation. The nobleman in our text made careful inquiries about the hour when his son was healed. It was by that information that he obtained his assurance. But we do not observe God's hand as much as we should. Our good, puritanic forefathers, when it rained, used to say that God had unstopped the bottles of heaven. When it rains today, we say that the clouds have become condensed. Our forefathers believed that God was concerned about the sunshine, the rain, the storms, the crops, and they were unashamed to plead with him about it. Today we speak of such things as laws of nature that must run their course. We fail to see the power behind the natural. We do not get our assurance because we do not observe enough. If we watched the providential goodness every day, if we noticed the answers to prayer, if we had a book of remembrances of God's graces toward us, we would become like this father who was led to full assurance of faith. He noticed that the very hour when Jesus spoke was the very hour of the healing. Be watchful, Christian. He who looks for providences will never lack a providence to observe.

Three Questions About Your Faith

You say, "I have faith." May it be so. But realize that there are many people who think they are rich but are actually poor. Does your faith make you pray? Not the praying of the man who prates like a parrot the prayers he has learned, but do you cry the cry of a living child? Do you tell God your needs and desires? And do you *seek* His face and *ask* His mercy? The person who can live without this type of prayer is a Christless soul. Faith is a delusion, and his confidence is a dream that will be destroyed. God cannot answer you if you are silent in your heart before Him. He who is never on his knees on earth shall never stand upon his feet in heaven. He who never wrestles with the Angel here below shall never be admitted into heaven by that Angel above. He who has true faith in his heart is praying all the day long. I do not mean on his knees, but whenever his heart finds a little space, a vacuum for a moment, it leaps into the bosom of God, then it is down again, refreshed to go about its business and meet the face of man. That is the way to live, and that is the life of a true believer. If your faith does not make you pray, get rid of it, and God help you to begin again in true faith.

I will ask a second question about your faith. Does that faith make you obedient? Jesus said to the nobleman, "Go thy way," and he went without a word. However much he might have wished to stay and listen to the Master or have the Master come with him, the nobleman obeyed. Does your faith make you obedient? I have heard of professing Christians who are not even honest and others who defile themselves with acts that many worldly people would scorn. I say that no Christian can act in business beneath the dignity of an honest man. If God has not made you honest, you are not saved in your soul. If you can disobey the moral laws of God, live inconsistently and lasciviously, and mix with the things that even an unbeliever might reject, the love of God is not in you. I do not plead for perfection, but I do plead for honesty. If your faith has not made you careful and prayerful in everyday life, it is an empty name, as sounding brass or a tinkling cymbal.

One more question and I will finish. Has your faith led you to bless your household? I have heard it said that when a man becomes a Christian, his dog and cat should be the better for it. A man should be a better husband, father, businessman, and worker than he was before, or else his religion is not genuine. A person who can keep his godliness to himself has so small a proportion of it that I am afraid it will be no credit to himself and no blessing to others. Faith that brings no passion for the saving of your family should be cast on the dunghill, hurled to the dogs, or buried in the graveyard. It is not the faith of God. "If any provide not for his own, and specially for those of his own house, he hath denied the faith, and is worse than an infidel" (1 Tim. 5:8).

Never be content until all your children are saved. Lay the promise before your God. The promise is for you and your children. The Greek word does not refer to infants but to children, grandchildren, and any descendants you have. I look back through four or five generations and see that God has been pleased to hear the prayers of our grandfather's grandfather, who prayed that his children might live before God to the last generation, and God has never deserted our house. So be it with you. God cannot refuse unless He runs back upon His promise. No matter how bad it looks, they are children that God has promised to bless. Pray that God will bring their eyes with sorrow to prayer, to supplication, to the cross, and to faith. Put your hand upon the Word of God and solemnly covenant with God that mercy be extended. He cannot refuse to give you both your own and your children's souls as an answer to the prayer of your faith.

*F*aith is the believer's highest and his lowest. If we ever get upon the mountain summit and bask our foreheads in the sunlight of fellowship with God, we shall stand there only by faith. It is because our faith is strong and active that we realize the things not seen as yet and behold the God whom mortal eyes cannot gaze upon. Our very noblest, happiest, and most heavenly frames are those that are the results of faith. And so in our lowest. We can live there only by faith. Have you never lain shattered and broken, crushed and destroyed, expecting something yet more terrible? And have you not felt that in your weakness you could fall back into the Savior's arms, that in your brokenness you could drop into His hand, that in your abject nothingness He must be all in all to you, or else there will be an utter end to you? Oh, the faith that is as wings to us when we fly becomes a lifebuoy to us when we sink! The faith that bears us up to the gates of heaven also uplifts us from the very gates of hell. It is all the senses of our spiritual nature from our highest or lowest. We must trust in the Lord.

Chapter Five

Faith Tried and Triumphing

Though he slay me, yet will I trust in him—Job 13:15.

THERE ARE SOME SPEECHES that could not be made by ordinary men. As soon as you hear one, you feel that there is a ring to it that is by no means common. Certain expressions that have been heard and remembered could have been uttered only by great warriors or men who have navigated the vast ocean. Other still nobler expressions could have been uttered only by those have had to fight with spiritual foes and have done business on the great waters of soul trouble. When you hear the expression, "If there are as many devils at Worms as there are tiles on the housetops, I will go there in God's name," you are quite certain the speaker is Martin Luther. None other than he could have said it. And as we consider the expression of Job, it seems to me that no one else could have uttered these words.

Job was a master sufferer. No man went deeper into grief than Job. His children all died, his wealth was swept away, his whole body was covered with sore boils and blisters, and the friends who pretended to comfort him only accused him of being a hypocrite. Even his own wife bid him "curse God, and die" (Job 2:9). He was brought lower than any, yet in the midst of his troubles we find his noble speech: "Though he slay me, yet will I trust in him." It is a sort of victorious word of faith that could come only from a triumphant Job. And it is from this expression that the believer's own faith may be increased.

Faith's Role in a Believer's Life

To trust in God is the normal mode of life for the believer. The believer does not sometimes trust and sometimes cease to trust, but "the just shall *live* by faith" (Rom. 1:17). Faith is not a grace of luxury but is a grace of necessity. We *must* have it to be the people of God. The common habit of the believer is a habit of trusting. The Christian's walk is faith, and his life is faith.

Faith is to the believer all the spiritual senses—not one but all. The natural man has his eyes, but by faith *we* see Him who is invisible. The natural man has his hand and his feeling. We live not by feeling, but our faith is the hand by which we take hold upon eternal realities. The natural man has his ear and is delighted with sweet sounds, but our faith is the ear through which we hear the voice of God and sometimes catch stray notes from the harps of the angels. The natural man has the nostril with which he is aware of sweet perfumes, but to our faith the name of Jesus is as the choicest ointment poured forth. If we receive Christ as our heart's Lord, all the inlets by which we receive Him and His grace are made the agate of faith. Gates of carbuncle, windows of agate, are true faith. The light of God and the love of God come into our consciousness by our faith.

Faith is with the Christian his first and his last. Faith looking to Christ is the very beginning of spiritual life. We began to live when at the cross we looked up and saw the flowing of those founts of forgiveness, the five wounds of Christ. And as faith was the first, so it will be the last. We expect to die looking for our Lord's appearing and resting upon His finished work. And all between the alpha and the omega, we read them all by faith. There is no period of our life in which it is safe for us to live by feelings, not even when our enjoyments run highest. On the mount where Christ is transfigured and where in the midst of the glory we shall fall asleep in amazement, we cannot live by our feelings. Even there we can enjoy the glory only as faith shall continue to be exercised. We must always look out of ourselves and look above to the things that are seen to grasp the things that are not seen, to be touched with the eternal hand, and realize that which does not seem real to our senses. This is the life of the Christian from the first to the last.

I would add that *faith is the believer's highest and his lowest*. If we ever get upon the mountain summit and bask our foreheads in the sunlight of fellowship with God, we shall stand there only by faith. It is because our faith is strong and active that we realize the things not seen as yet and behold the God whom mortal eyes cannot gaze upon. Our very noblest, happiest, and most heavenly frames are those that are the results of faith. And so in our lowest. We can live there only by faith. Have you never lain shattered and broken, crushed and destroyed, expecting something yet more terrible? And have you not felt that in your weakness you could fall back into the Savior's arms, that in your brokenness you could drop into His hand, that in your abject nothingness He must be all in all to you, or else there will be an utter end to you? Oh, the faith that is as wings to us when we fly becomes a lifebuoy to us when we sink! The faith that bears us up to the gates of heaven also uplifts us from the very gates of hell. It is all the senses of our spiritual nature from our highest or lowest. We *must* trust in the Lord.

The matters about which the Christian is to trust are very many, but they are primarily the ones that follow.

We trust for the pardon of our sins to our God in Christ Jesus. The *only* hope that any believer has for the forgiveness of his iniquity lies in the sacrifice presented on Calvary by the Lamb of God whom God has given for the sins of the world. In this matter we can use the language of Job and say, "Though he slay me, yet will I trust in him," for the fact is, the more fully we are slain, the more truly we do trust. When we see ourselves to be utterly dead, slain by the two-edged sword of the Lord, and all hope of our own self-salvation to be a corpse, then it is easier than before to come and cast ourselves upon the Christ of God and rest there.

But in God *we trust also for the purification of our spirits* from all the indwelling power of sin. Some believers fail to make this a matter of faith. You can no more conquer sin in yourself than you can remove the guilt of it by your own merits. The same Christ who is made "justification" and "redemption" is also made to us "sanctification" (1 Cor. 1:30), and we must not forget it. The same

Savior who takes away the guilt also takes away the defiling power of sin. The believer does not hope to drive out one of these Canaanites by his own strength. But his eyes are unto the hills from where his help comes, and he believes that the eternal Spirit will go through and through his soul like a refining fire till everything in him shall be burned up except that which is pleasing to God. We trust the blessed Spirit to sanctify us, spirit, soul, and body.

Our trust in God is shown in other ways as well. *We trust Him, believing that He always must be just.* It does not occur to us now that God could be unjust. In the days of our flesh, we used to think that God had dealt very harshly with us if we suffered extreme pain or passed from wealth to poverty. Today it does not occur to us in any way to impeach the justice of God but to simply let Him do what He will. We feel that if He should slay us, we should not complain against Him. Our firm confidence is that He never will deal unjustly with us.

Having believed in Christ and become His children, *we trust that God will never do anything to us but that which is full of love.* We are assured that His eternal love does not come forth only now and then, but that all His conduct toward His children is actuated by the motive power of love. He is always love toward those who put their trust in Him. We are sure that He never gives us a pain more than is needful, that He never allows us to suffer a loss more than is necessary. "Though for a season, if need be, ye are in heaviness through manifold temptations" (1 Pet. 1:6), we know and are convinced that there *is* a "need be" for it. We trust His justice and His goodness.

Moreover, *we trust His wisdom mingled with all this.* He has said that "all things work together for good to them that love God, to them who are called according to his purpose" (Rom. 8:28), and we believe it. We have tasted life's bitterness, yet we still believe it. We may yet taste much more, yet we are assured that through the help of God's Spirit we shall still believe this. Come what may, expected or unexpected, in the ways of grief and sorrow, still we believe that ultimate good will come out of the whole. God's purpose of love shall not be thwarted but rather shall be answered by every circumstance of our history. God is wise, loving, and just, and He cannot do an untender thing to us.

Finally, *we trust Him as a child trusts its parent,* that is, for everything. There are many things about Him that we cannot understand, as there were about our parents in our childhood, but we trust Him and know that there is none like Him. "Who is like unto thee, O LORD, among the gods? Who is like thee, glorious in holiness, fearful in praises, doing wonders?" (Exod. 15:11). We cannot understand Him, but we are sure that His footsteps are of holiness and His ways of righteousness. We trust Him for the past, the present, and the future. That future that looms before us in the mist and half alarms us till we are ready to shrink back from it. We gather up the skirts of our robe again, and though we fear as we enter into the cloud, yet we are comforted with the full conviction that He who has done so well in the past will be with us even to life's close.

Our Faith Shall Be Tried

Believers expect that their faith shall be tried. From Job we learn that it shall be tried extremely. Job does not say, "Though I *die*," which is a great trial by itself. He does say, "Though he *slay* me." That is much more. It is not about being allowed to go hungry, or put in prison, or to suffer mockery, or to be banished from our friends, or even to be slain by others. "Though he slay me" comes right home to my own self.

Job knew what he meant, for everything else had been done except the slaying of himself. His children were dead, and the house in which they had met was in ruin. All he possessed was gone. His health was gone, and he could not rest by reason of the disease that was all over him, most painful and most acute. He was even friendless; and he was worse than wifeless, for his wife had turned against him. Yet, he says, there is but one thing more that can be done, and God has kept Satan back from that. God said, "Save his life" (Job 2:6), and Job's faith was willing for that to go as well.

The text implies that *faith will be tried, and tried severely*. Has it not always been the case that if any person has had a faith beyond his fellows, it has met with trial. If you step beyond the ordinary rank and files, you will be shot at for that very reason. Columbus believed that there was another part of the world undiscovered, and see the ridicule heaped upon him. Galileo said the world moves and was put into the inquisition. It can be dangerous to know too much or to believe a little more than others. And in spiritual things, it is just the same. The world is against the true faith. The faith of God's elect is not a flower that men delight to admire and praise. This world is not of faith, and the darkness that is in the world will try to quench its light.

But remember that *true faith scorns trial and outlives it*. Faith is not worth having if it does not. If I believe in the friendship of my friend, and yet it cannot bear a little trial, it is not real friendship. Real faith believes his God when God begins to take away the things he loves. Job's faith remained when everything of temporal value was stripped from him. This is faith worth having. But if faith cannot continue to believe in the hard things, it is not the faith that is worthy of God. If it does give way, it will hopefully drive the man to seek the true faith that bears the tests.

Turn over the historical pages of the Bible and discover that all the Lord's children have had to do battle for the preservation of their faith. Follow the annals of the church's history and find that the best servants of God have had their trials. And why should we expect to escape. There is no smooth road to heaven. Heavy road equipment can be used for the roads built today, but we find the flint stones on the road to glory. They have never been rolled smooth yet, and they never will be. Do not run away from trials, but do not run after trouble either. Leave the trials to the hand of God. Do not fret yourself there. In our peace of soul, whatever God brings to us is the road for us to walk. But realize that some thorns and thistles must and will spring up in this present world.

Moreover, *the trial is greatly for our good and greatly for God's glory*. Our faith could never grow, neither could we be sure of it, if it had not been tested. God tries us here, before we take the great ocean of judgment at death. We have our trials here, and we grow by our trials. Among the best mercies we have ever received are those mercies that come to us dressed in the garb of mourning. God be thanked for the fire! God be thanked for the refiner's furnace and the crucible! They have been among the best things we have inherited from His mercy.

True Faith Bears Trial

When put on trial, a true faith will certainly bear it. "Though he slay me." It is an extreme expression. "Though He do His worst, though He give the last and uttermost stroke that can be taken, yet I will not disbelieve Him."

Faith will be justified to the uttermost. While it is easy to believe the creature too much, it is impossible to trust the Creator too much. To trust Him too little is one of the most usual of sins. Faith in the Creator can be pushed as far as you like. You know that there is a point where faith in the creature must stop. Our dearest friends can go with us only to the Jordan's brink, and then they can help us no longer. But though we go through the valley of the shadow of death, God is with us, and we need fear no evil. Still we trust Him. He will not fail us.

Why is it that the believer is warranted in trusting in God to the very last extremity? Because He is always the same God. If He is worth trusting one day, He is worth trusting another. He cannot change. His character is such that if it is infinitely worthy of my confidence today, it will be just the same in the rough weather that may come tomorrow. Could He change, then my faith in Him ought to change. But if He is ever the same true, faithful, loving, and tender God, ruling all things by His power, there can be no reason why my faith should make a change.

I should trust Him also to the finish because *outward providences prove nothing to us about God.* We cannot read outward events any better than we can read hieroglyphics. The Book is written in human language, but the works of God are often unreadable. If the Lord says that He loves us, we believe it though it appears that He smites us. Be wise, then, and believe in the God whom you cannot see and not in the outward providence that you can see. If you could see the outward providence correctly, you would see it to be full of love as assuredly as God's heart is. However black the outward sign may be, still let us believe Him. When it shall seem most severe, let us still hope in Him.

There is another cause why we should always trust in Him. *To whom else can we go?* When it comes to slaying, what can the soul do but fall into the Creator's arms? When it comes to dying, what words shall fit these lips so well as those: "Father, into thy hands I commend my spirit" (Luke 23:46). The course of the Christian's life is such that he feels it more necessary to trust every day he lives. He does not get off the line of faith but sets more into the middle of it, as he feels his weakness more and more. He says, "My flesh and my heart faileth: but God is the strength of my heart, and my portion for ever" (Ps. 73:26). When all other sources are dried up and the world mocks us, it seems to be a howling wilderness. To whom else should we go in our trouble but to God?

We may depend upon it that *God will always justify our faith* if we do trust Him. There was never one who in the long run had to say, "I was a fool to trust in God." God has not left the righteous to be ashamed and offended forever. Faith has come to the rescue, and God has fulfilled their faith. Many a man has trusted himself and been deceived; many have trusted their wealth and been disappointed; many have relied on friends and been betrayed, but blessed is the man who makes the Lord his trust. You can never ask too much of His hands or expect too much. Has He not said, "I am the LORD thy God, which brought thee out of the land of Egypt: open thy mouth wide, and I will fill it" (Ps. 81:10). The wider you open it, the better; the larger your expectations of God, the better, for according to your faith it will done unto you.

For faith to be true it will *require the power of God Himself.* Recall that God does not care for our words. It is the heart, it is the reality and truth of what we say that commends us to Him. Many boast religiously about their faith, but a sickness or a loss comes and their faith wavers. A little puff of wind will alter some people's faith. Oh, for a faith that is strengthened by God to stand the test! Seek such a faith from the Strong One. Say, "Lord, I believe; help my unbelief, and bring me to this, that I can look anything in the face." God will keep to the end those who have rested in Him.

The man who believes without seeing is truly blessed because he is having a grand character formed in him. It is a poor character who lives only on what he sees. There is no great character that can ever come to a man who has no faith. The heroes among men are all men of faith, even those who are heroes concerning common matters. It was faith of some sort that braced them up and made them superior to those around them. No one could be a William Tell who had no firm confidence. And no man could have been a Martin Luther who was not completely trusting his God. What a wondrous thing to be driven out from paddling our canoe of faith along the shore when by a big rolling wave we are carried right out to sea, and there to be taught to be a mariner who braves the tempest and laughs at the hurricane. We would always remain children if we did not have trials and troubles. God often hides Himself in order to teach us to trust Him more, and so we grow to be men of faith.

Chapter Six

Faith Without Sight

Jesus saith unto him, Thomas, because thou hast seen me, thou hast believed: blessed are they that have not seen, and yet have believed—John 20:29.

WHAT A PRIVILEGE AND BLESSING it was for those people who lived in our Savior's day and saw Him when He dwelt here among men. Their eyes saw and their ears heard what kings and prophets had long desired to see and hear yet were not so privileged. But we who now believe in our Lord Jesus Christ have a blessing superior to theirs, for the benediction of the text is to those who "have not seen, and yet have believed." No doubt Thomas was highly favored when the Lord said to him, "Reach hither thy finger, and behold my hands; and reach hither thy hand, and thrust it into my side" (John 20:27). This was such a remarkable condescension on Christ's part that I can hardly imagine any other of the twelve apostles being more tenderly treated than this doubting disciple. Yet as privileged as Thomas was, the Master proclaims a superior blessing to us: "Blessed are they that have not seen, and yet have believed."

How often do we say in our hearts, "What a blessing to be in heaven where they behold Christ face to face. The saints and angels see the King in His beauty in the land that is so far off." Yes, there's no doubting that they are truly blessed, for John heard the voice from heaven saying, "Write, Blessed are the dead which die in the Lord from henceforth" (Rev. 14:13). There is indescribable bliss for all those who behold their Savior's face and wear His name on their foreheads. But we are mistaken to think that all blessedness is reserved for the glorified, for we have much here also. Jesus' words to Thomas almost seem like He had commenced to preach His Sermon on the Mount again or to add another beatitude: "blessed are they that have not seen, and yet have believed." The day will come when with our eyes we shall see Christ in His glory, but for now it is quite enough to fill us to the very brim with joy if we can take in the full meaning of the Master's words.

Do Not Allow This Blessing to Diminish

Jesus was clear that we have a special blessing through not having seen and yet having believed, so do not diminish it by *desiring a voice or a vision or a revelation*—things that are based on sight. Perhaps you have said to yourself, "Oh, but if God would in some way reveal Himself to me so that my senses might assist my faith. If I could but hear some divine whisper that I am His or just get a glimpse of His glory, I would never doubt again. If I could see some miracle occur, something that I was sure was the finger of God, or get near enough to God to be impressed for life, what a grand thing that would be!" You do not feel content to swim in the pure sea of faith, but your Lord will not give you what you childishly crave. He instead says, "My child, instead of wanting to see, believe, trust, follow me in the dark, for it is better for you not to see. Even if you did see, you would only obtain an inferior gift, for the higher blessing is for those who have not seen and yet have believed."

Next, when you are in trouble, do not diminish the blessing *by asking for some remarkable and special providence to open to you*. God's providence is always at work, and we make mistakes in putting down some things as providences and others as not. You escape in a railway accident and say it is providence. Yet it is just as much a providence that you go to town six days a week without any accident. To be supplied bread when you are out of work is no greater providence than to not lose your work and not be in need. I do not say that you are not to pray for providence to help you, but I urge you not to be continually pining after those special providences that are picked out of some men's biographies. Do not say, "I expect God to do something wonderful for me or I cannot trust Him." No, "blessed are they that have not seen, and yet have believed." The blessing is for those who through the whole of their lives know that the right hand of God has been leading them steadily on. Though there is nothing they could write about as a sort of semi-miracle, yet they believe that all things are working together for good for them.

Again, do not diminish the blessing *by craving after ecstatic experiences.* It is a very delightful thing to have your soul made like a heavenly chariot and to be carried away with holy delights. Such sacred joys have been given to many saints. Paul wrote about his own experience: "whether in the body, I cannot tell; or whether out of the body, I cannot tell" (2 Cor. 12:2). Those are happy seasons with special delight, but we must not say, "I cannot trust in God because I have no such experience." Oh, no! Trust Him even if it is pitch black around you. Rely upon Him though you cannot see a star in the night. Though you have not even had any spiritual joy arising out of the conscious possession of divine life in your soul, still cling to Him whose everlasting arm has never failed any clinging soul and whose lovingkindnesses and tender mercies are just as sure in the darkest night as in the brightest day.

There is another way in which we may diminish this blessing of faith without sight: *by always demanding clear arguments to answer every objection that may be raised.* How often through the years have I heard of some great discovery that would undermine the very foundations of our faith. When I was a boy, the great arguments against the Scriptures were founded upon the stones dug out of the earth. Geology had come up, and therefore Christianity was to go down! Since then, any number of remarkable things have come and gone. Some have been considerably shaken and troubled. Let us hear our Lord saying to us, "Blessed are they that have not seen, and yet have believed." Let us come to the point that we know what we know, and it is divinely fixed in our soul that it is so. If an objection is raised against what we believe, we feel certain that it will be answered. It may not be our duty to answer it, and we may not have the special knowledge that is necessary for that task.

Nowadays it seems to be the business of a great many learned fools to find difficulties for wise men to answer. We have something else to do beside answering them. If you try to satisfy every man who starts a new theory, you have nothing to do but to answer objections. Things like proving the presence of the Holy Spirit in your soul must be so truly a matter of personal consciousness that whatever argument may be urged against it, you may say, "I know that the Father has begotten a new life in me that I never had till His blessed Spirit wrought it in me. I know that He has lifted me up into a new world and has given me to see and know what I never even dreamed of until I came to trust Him. That is my answer." It may not satisfy an objector, but it may satisfy yourself.

We may diminish this blessing *by being overanxious for success in our work*. We should be anxious to win souls for the Lord Jesus Christ, but blessed is the man who goes on faithfully preaching the gospel when no one is converted. Blessed is he who believes in the power of the gospel, though for the moment it is not manifest to him. Keep on believing and crying to God for their salvation.

We must not diminish this blessing *by wanting always to have the concurrent faith of others to support our own*. There are some people who can believe while everybody around them believes. They feel bright and happy if others come and cheer them. Theirs is a kind of seeing by proxy—somebody else sees, so you believe. But blessed is he who has not seen, even with other people's eyes, and yet has believed. Blessed is he who says, "I can stand alone. If there is nobody else who believes the truth, I know it is true. I rest in the truth of Scripture. Let others go whatever way they will. I stand steadfastly for God, and my faith shall not be shaken." This is a blessed way of living.

This Blessedness Is Attainable

If we are believers in Jesus Christ, let us believe that it is possible for us to believe without seeing, for *God deserves to be believed*. Apart from every other consideration, His own personal character is such that He should be believed. If God has spoken to us in the Scriptures and revealed a truth that has no analogy in nature, that is not supported by the judgment of learned men, and to which our own experience seems to be in contradiction, still God must be believed. The fact that God has said it should weigh down the scales of our understanding. Surely you are not going to set the evidence of your eyes against the declaration of God who cannot lie. I am determined that if all my senses contradict God, I would rather deny every one of them than believe that God could lie. I desire to feel that in every emotion of my spirit, every throb of my heart, every thought of my brain, and in everything that is contrary to the plainly revealed truth of God, I will reckon God to be wise and true. If we trust Him as He should be trusted, we shall realize the blessedness of which our text speaks.

Further, look along the whole line of history, *note how the saints have trusted in the Lord*, and see whether He has not been true to them. From the days of Noah to the coming of Christ, trace the inspired record and see what it will prove to you. Has He said something that He has not done? Has He promised and ever failed to keep His word? Has He threatened and failed to carry out the threat? Look through the biographies of all who have trusted Him. Has He deceived any of them? Has it ever been shown to be foolish to believe God? The whole roll of the past confirms the faithfulness of God.

I appeal to you who have believed in God and ask *if your own experience has not warranted your faith*. How has He treated you? Has He ever given you any occasion to distrust Him? Any reason to suspect the faithfulness of God? I have sometimes called myself ten thousand thousand fools in one for ever doubting the faithfulness of God. When I look back over my own life, it always seems as remarkable as anything that has ever been found in the pages of fiction. How wonderfully and graciously God has dealt with me! What do I not owe to His faithfulness and truth? Doubt You, my Lord? I could doubt all except You, and doubt myself most of all. In deep waters, in sickness, in poverty, in sorrow, in depression, through fire and through water, we discover the mercy of God. Yes, He deserves to be trusted although we cannot see Him.

Do Not Miss This Blessing

It is a blessed thing to trust God when you cannot see, for *this is a sure mark of a spiritual and renewed mind*. There were many who saw Christ and still cried, "Crucify Him." There were some who saw His wonderful power and yet did not believe. Some people even believed in Him in some sense but would not follow as a disciple. Believing without seeing is the evidence that you are a child of God. "Whom having not seen, ye love; in whom, though now ye see him not, yet believing, ye rejoice with joy unspeakable and full of glory: Receiving the end of your faith, even the salvation of your souls" (1 Pet. 1:8–9). If that describes your faith, you may make certain of your election and adoption into the Lord's family.

This kind of man is blessed because *believing when he has not seen is a proof that his heart is right toward God*. When we trust someone, we believe that what they say is true simply because they have said it. And when you trust God in spite of all outward appearances and surrounding circumstances, it is a comfortable proof to yourself that you are on good terms with God and that you are walking in sweet fellowship with Him. Even when the Lord disciplines us and our heart is heavy with discouragement, still we can say with Job, "Though he slay me, yet will I trust in him" (Job 13:15).

Those who believe Christ whom they have not seen are blessed *because their character and conduct in this respect are most acceptable with God*. I do not know anything that gratifies a man more than to be implicitly trusted. There are not many of us who are worthy of such confidence. When people do absolutely trust us, we feel that they have given us all the honor that they can possibly put on us. And our Lord delights for us just to give ourselves up to trust him in that fashion. I do not believe that the seraphim in heaven praise the Lord so much in all their hallelujahs as a tried child of God does when he trusts himself entirely in his Heavenly Father's hands. And it seems to me that the darker the night and the heavier the burden and the more crushed the spirit, if we can fully trust Him then, the sweeter is the music of our resignation and the more acceptable the homage that we pay to God. It is a wonderful thing that we poor creatures can by any means be able to give pleasure to the infinitely happy God. Yet we do so when we trust Him.

You will find that the man who believes without seeing is truly blessed *because that faith brings comfort to his own soul*. I have never been so happy in all my life as when I have had nothing to trust but God. The times when I have been flung into the sea and compelled to swim because I could not touch the bottom have been the most joyous times to my own heart. In the times when I have been enabled to just believe God and to leave everything in His hands, I have seen the Lord's hand working marvelously in the midst of the earth, and it has given me the utmost delight. Happiness is not found when the barns are full and the vats are running over. Happiness is knowing that whatever you have, the Lord is your provider. You cannot have a better provider.

Another reason why such a person is blessed is that *he is having a grand character formed in him.* It is a poor character who lives only on what he sees. There is no great character that can ever come to a man who has no faith. The heroes among men are all men of faith, even those who are heroes concerning common matters. It was faith of some sort that braced them up and made them superior to those around them. No one could be a William Tell who had no firm confidence. And no man could have been a Martin Luther who was not completely trusting his God. What a wondrous thing to be driven out from paddling our canoe of faith along the shore when by a big rolling wave we are carried right out to sea, and there to be taught to be a mariner who braves the tempest and laughs at the hurricane. We would always remain children if we did not have trials and troubles. God often hides Himself in order to teach us to trust Him more, and so we grow to be men of faith.

Let me remind you that *we are very likely coming to a time when we shall need to believe without the use of our eyes.* If our Lord Jesus Christ does not come soon, we shall die. And if your faith depends on your sight, what will you do when your eyes are in the grave? Do not always be wanting to use these poor eyeballs, for they do not see much. There are angels flying nearby where you are reading. I cannot see them with these eyes, but I shall see them when these eyes are gone. Our Lord is also with us, but I cannot see Him either. I am soon to come to live in a world where I will have no hands or eyes or ears until the resurrection morning. I must learn to know God apart from sight. If you want to enjoy great blessings and lead a happy life and die a triumphant death, if you would see your Master's face with acceptance in the day of His appearing, ask that this blessing may be yours now: "Blessed are they that have not seen, and yet have believed."

If you start on the voyage of life by divine grace and the resolve that you will follow the track marked down on the chart by the Lord your God, you will find that you have chosen a course that the Lord's hand alone can keep you true. The current does not run that way. Before long you will find that the wind is dead against you and the course to be followed is hard to keep. When duty is contrary to your temperament or feelings, what will you do then if you have no faith? When it involves loss of money or ease or honor, what will you do then? If you believe that God is the Rewarder of them who diligently seek Him, you will persevere, but not otherwise. Suppose the right course should expose you to ridicule, cause you to be spoken of as a fanatic or mocked at as a hypocrite or despised as a fool, what can you do without faith? If your faith fails you, self love will create such respect for your own good name, such fear of ridicule, such unwillingness to stand alone, that you will slide from your integrity and choose a smooth and pleasing road.

Chapter Seven

The Best Strengthening Medicine

Out of weakness were made strong—Hebrews 11:34.

THOSE WHO OUT OF WEAKNESS were made strong are written among the heroes of faith in Hebrews 11. Believers "quenched the violence of fire, escaped the edge of the sword, out of weakness were made strong." Who shall tell which of the three grand deeds of faith is the greatest? Many of us may never have to brave the fiery stake or die the cruel death that Paul did. But if we have grace enough to be made strong out of weakness, we shall not be left out of the roll of the nobles of faith, and God's name shall not fail to be glorified in our lives.

As believers in the Lord Jesus, *we are called to two things*: to do and to suffer for His name's sake. Certain saints are summoned to active marching duty, and others are ordered to keep watch on the walls. There are warriors on the field of conflict and sentries in the box of patience.

Both in doing and in suffering, if we are observant, *we soon discover our own weakness*. "Weakness" is all we possess. It meets us everywhere. If we have to work for the Lord, we are soon compelled to cry, "Who is sufficient for these things?" (2 Cor. 2:16). But if we are called to suffer for Him, our weakness is often even greater. Many who can labor without weariness cannot suffer without impatience. Men are seldom equally skilled in the use of the two hands of doing and bearing. Patience is a grace that is rarer and harder to find than activity and zeal. It is one of the choicest fruits of the Spirit and seldom found on newly planted trees. The fact soon comes home to us that we are weak where we most of all desire to be strong.

Whether to do or to suffer for our Lord, *we must have strength from above, and that strength can come to us only through faith.* The remarkable mighty saints of Hebrews 11 accomplished all their feats by a power that was not in them by nature. They were not naturally strong either to do or to suffer. If they had been, they would not have required faith in God. They were quite as weak as the weakest of us, but by their faith they laid hold on heavenly strength until they could do all things. There was nothing in the range of impossibility that they could not have performed. They achieved everything that was necessary in the form of service, and they bore up gloriously under the most fearful pressure of suffering, simply and only by faith in God who became their Helper. They proved that *we can be made strong out of just such weakness.* We need not desire to have any strength of our own, for by faith we can reach to any degree of power in the Lord. We can have all imaginable strength for the grandest achievements desirable if we have faith in God.

We all wish to be strong spiritually. From the example of those who "out of weakness were made strong" we can learn to be made strong as well.

Faith Makes Men Strong for Holy Work

The first duty of a Christian is *to obey God.* Obedience is hard work to proud flesh and blood. Indeed, ingrained rebels will never obey through their own efforts. We love our own will and way, and it goes against the grain to bring ourselves into such complete subjection as the law of the Lord requires. "Thou shalt love the Lord thy God with all thy heart, and with all thy soul, and with all thy strength, and with all thy mind" (Luke 10:27). Who among us has done this? Faith alone takes hold of the divine strength, and only by that strength can we obey. Hence, faith is the essential point of holiness.

If you start on the voyage of life by divine grace and the resolve that you will follow the track marked down on the chart by the Lord your God, you will find that you have chosen a course that the Lord's hand alone can keep you true. The current does not run that way. Before long you will find that the wind is dead against you and the course to be followed is hard to keep. When duty is contrary to your temperament or feelings, what will you do then if you have no faith? When it involves loss of money or ease or honor, what will you do then? If you believe that God is the Rewarder of them who diligently seek Him, you will persevere, but not otherwise. Suppose the right course should expose you to ridicule, cause you to be spoken of as a fanatic or mocked at as a hypocrite or despised as a fool, what can you do without faith? If your faith fails you, self love will create such respect for your own good name, such fear of ridicule, such unwillingness to stand alone, that you will slide from your integrity and choose a smooth and pleasing road.

Though you may think it a very ordinary thing to obey God in all things, you will find you need to set your face like a flint to keep to the road. The only way to hold to your way is by faith in God. If you say, "God commands, and therefore I must do it," you will be strong. If you believe that God will bear you through, you will be strong. If you believe that God will reward your faith, you will be strong. We are not saved *by* obedience, for obedience is the result of salvation. Faith is weakness clinging to strength and becoming strong through so doing. Faith in God caused the cripple at the temple gate to stand and walk and leap and praise God. Even so, faith makes our sin-crippled manhood obey the will of the Lord with exaltation.

Faith makes us strong *to fulfill the relationships of life*. We are not alone, for God has lined us with others. We either curse or bless those around us. If we have faith in God, we shall bless our children as Isaac and Jacob blessed their sons. Faith leaves a legacy of benediction to its heirs. By faith you may bless your brothers while you live, as Joseph did. By faith you can lead others out of the bondage of sin and through the wilderness world, as Moses led the children of Israel. But without faith you cannot bless others. To the wife who has a godless husband, I say have faith in God about him. Do not try to convert him apart from heavenly power. Parent, are your children unruly, unspiritual, and defiant? Go to God in prayer and faith. A parent can do serious damage with his children by his very efforts to do them good. One parent is too indulgent, another is too severe. Take the children to God. It is here that your strength lies. Strength to do right at the head of a household must come by divine gift, and that gift will only be placed in the open hand of faith. If we believe for our whole house, the promise will be fulfilled to us and to our children.

Perhaps you fear God and live in an ungodly home. Do you feel bewildered as to how to behave yourself? Orders are given you that cause you great heart searchings. Or you question in your inmost soul whether you can conscientiously do as your employer requires. Have faith in God that He will direct you and have faith to follow that direction when you receive it. To take a stand that is firm and steadfast for God makes a man out of a boy, and his after years will be bright and useful. But if he begins to give way a little, trimming his sail to the wind, he will never attain a holy character. That which begins with shamefacedness, hesitation, and compromise will ripen into apostasy. Such a wretched faith has no influence on the man's self, and it will have no influence upon others. If you feel weak in the carrying out of your duty, exercise your faith in God about it, and out of weakness you shall be made strong.

There is a high and blessed privilege that every Christian has as a necessity of life, and that is *to pray*. If you know how to pray, you can move heaven and earth. You can set almighty forces in operation. But you say, "I cannot pray in a way that prevails with God." You say you are not like Jacob who took hold upon the angel and won the victory (Gen. 32:24–32). You feel so weak in prayer. Well, then, let me bring the text before you. Out of this weakness in prayer you can be made strong only *by faith*. Believe in God, and you will prevail with God. Believe in His promise and plead it. Believe in His Spirit and pray by His help. Believe in Jesus who makes intercession for you, for through Him you may come boldly to the throne of grace. Faith alone can strengthen weak knees. "According to your faith be it unto you."

To pray without faith is formality and vanity. To be weak in prayer is a disease that will bring on many other diseases. He who knows how to pray has his hand on the lever that moves the universe. But there is no praying without believing. If you believe, you shall be heard, for God refuses no believing prayer. We have this strong confidence: "He that spared not his own Son, but delivered him up for us all, how shall he not with him also freely give us all things?" (Rom. 8:32). Jesus said, "If ye then, being evil, know how to give good gifts unto your children, how much more shall your Father which is in heaven give good things to them that ask him?" (Matt. 7:11). Prayer makes "rich towards God," and this is the best of riches. But it must be believing prayer. "But let him ask in faith, nothing wavering" (James 1:6).

Faith is also the great force that is needed by those whose principal work is *to overcome sin*. When God began with many of us, He found us very low down beneath the flood of evil. Perhaps it was an awful temper that broke over us in surging waves. We have to rise superior to it. Possibly He found us plunged in the great deeps of an evil habit. It had to be left beneath so we could rise out of it. When God begins with many people, a desperate ascent even to reach common morality occurs. What must the conflict be before they attain to spirituality and holiness?

It is hard for those to rise to the surface who have been plunged in the deeps. For a man who has been sunk down in black waters full of filth a thousand fathoms deep, and if he has been imprisoned in dark caves where no light has come, what a wondrous power would that be that should raise him to the sunlight! What a work of the Spirit of God to bring him up from the horrible midnight and to give him strength to rise out of the ilky waters! I have seen many a soul wearying to ascent, receiving a little light and a little more light, but yet far from being clear of the dark waters of iniquity.

You will never overcome sin except by faith in Christ Jesus. Trust Him! Trust in the precious blood that kills sin. Trust His pierced hands to pierce the hands of your lusts. Trust His wounded side to smite through the heart of your evil desires. Your hope lies there: where Jesus died, where Jesus rose again, where Jesus has gone into the glory. You may resolve to overcome a sin and perhaps conquer it for a time. But sin itself is a forceful army that will never be overcome except through the blood of the Lamb. God can strengthen you out of weakness to overcome sin, though it is backed by the world, the flesh, and the devil. However deeply entrenched sin may be in your nature, you will drive out the Canaanites and free your heart from their dominion.

I have often met with persons awakened by divine grace who have said, "I do not know how I will ever break this evil habit," yet they have very easily escaped from it through repentance and faith. Other sins cling to a man like the fabled tunic of Hercules that could not be torn away but burned into his flesh and bone no matter what he did. How long a beloved habit lingers at the door after the heart has given it notice to get out! As a dog that is chased away from the house may return again and again to its former owner, so does an evil lust turn again even to the soul that hates it. How weak we are in this matter! How slow to cut it off! But it must be done, and only faith in the Almighty's help can do it. Trust in Christ to overcome by His Spirit that which He has put away by His death. Out of weakness you will be made strong by faith.

Faith is required for the Christian to effectively *spread the gospel*. Many are well aware of their duty to tell others about what Christ has done in their life but feel very timid about it. We are apt to attempt to share the good news in our own strength, and then we wonder if we break down. If we were by faith to humbly wait upon the Lord for words and take hold upon divine strength, might we not accomplish far more than we do now? Let us not fear that we will break down. If you are sincere, you might do more by a breakdown than by anything else. Only break the ice and begin. You may find that out of weakness you will be made strong. God does not need your strength. He has more than enough power of His own. He asks for your weakness, and He is longing to take it as the instrument in His own mighty hand.

Perhaps you would like *to do something great for God*. Have you heard the motto of our early missionaries: "Attempt great things for God." Does that thought burn within your heart? Do you desire to be used by God? "Oh, yes," you say, "but I am terribly weak." Make the attempt by faith in the God who can make you strong. Throw yourself upon the infinite capacity of God. As long as you are willing to be used, as long as God has given you a travail in spirit for the soul of others, you need not fear. Has not the Lord said, "My grace is sufficient for thee: for my strength is made perfect in weakness" (2 Cor. 12:9)? And is not that word true?

I would make one more application about our weakness being made strong. This will be experienced *in bearing witness for the faith of God*. Suppose that you are called to testify for truth in the midst of those who doubt, disbelieve, or even deride it. You look at those who agree with you, and they are lukewarm. You turn to old friends, and they do not share your concerns. People say that you are narrow-minded and bigoted in religion. Faith can turn these bullets into pellets and the stones as soft as sponges. You need not bristle up and vindicate yourself. God will vindicate His own cause, but it may be His way to let error and lies prevail for a while. Bide your time when the cause is an eternal one, for you can afford to do so.

If we had been in Egypt at the time when Pharaoh started out to follow the Israelites to the Red Sea, we would have taken off their chariot wheels before they could get under way. But Jehovah did something better. He allowed the Egyptians to pursue and overtake and threaten, and then He allowed them in their pride to go down after Israel into the depths of the sea. When He overthrew them, Israel could sing, "The horse and his rider hath he thrown into the sea" (Exod. 15:1). This was a grand thing for the tribes in their journeys through the wilderness to come. They need never fear Pharaoh again. Meanwhile, the tremendous blow made their future antagonists in Canaan tremble. In the conflict with evil, we would overcome it early and put it to rout at the first attack. But it may be that God will allow error to proceed further and let it seem to triumph, so that by its own presumption it may place itself where it is more effectually crushed, never again to afflict the church. It is for us in our weakness to go forward as the Lord leads us. The day of the resounding timbrels will come in due time, and Jehovah will be magnified with the saints as they "sing unto the LORD, for he hath triumphed gloriously" (Exod. 15:1). Be steadfast, immovable. Never mind the lies, the criticisms, and the number of the foe. God's time is best. He knows better than we do when to strike for victory. Out of weakness we shall be made strong if we rely on faith.

Faith Makes Men Strong for Patient Suffering

Many believers are called upon to suffer much *in daily life*. What a world of misery there is in this great city. The poverty of even godly people in London would be a subject too harrowing for those who have tender hearts. Few believers are without sorrow, and many saints have a double portion of grief in their pilgrimage. Your life may be one protracted struggle for existence. You endure in the faith only "as seeing him who is invisible" (Heb. 11:27). You must find joy in God, or you will not find joy at all. Earthly comforts are not yours, but as you grasp the spiritual and eternal, you will not complain. If in this life only you had hope, you would be of all men most miserable, but having that hope, you are among the most happy. Commend me to firm faith for power to bear the daily cross. He who believes has everlasting life and the joys that come with it. Trust in the care of your God and you shall be as the lilies that neither toil nor spin and yet are clothed, or as the ravens, which have no store and yet are fed. Heaven is prepared for you, empowering you to defy cold, hunger, nakedness, shame, and everything else in this world. Your faith out of weakness shall make you strong.

Certain believers are called to bear *great physical pain*, and I commend to them the power of faith in God under acute agony. This is the sweetest support in the presence of a physical suffering. Go not to wine for comfort in the hour of depression. Do not appeal to friends for consolation. What do they know of your inward sorrow? There are seas of suffering that the sufferer must navigate alone. No other sail is within sight. Scan the horizon, and nothing is to be seen but wave after wave. Now is the hour for faith in the great Lord, who holds even lonely seas in the hollow of His hand. He knows your poor body, and He permits it to be afraid. He permits your heart to be trembling because He will glorify Himself in His tenderness to your weakness. "I am the LORD that healeth thee" (Exod. 15:26). Give yourself to Him, and you shall yet sing of His lovingkindness and tender mercies.

But there are other forms of suffering than these of daily life and bodily pain. Possibly you are suffering the evils of *persecution*. It may not be at the hands of a cruel tyrant, but there are ways enough for the seed of the serpent to show its enmity to the seed of the woman. "Trials of cruel mockings" are still common. There are many ways in which the devil's whip can reach the back of the child of God. There are households of martyrdom where a godly wife must contend with the jeering of her husband or of a godly youth who endures scoffing and far worse. For those who suffer, may the Lord keep you from anger and unkindness. By faith alone can you bear persecution and turn it to account for the good of others. Ask the Lord to help you to stand fast for Him. Not now do I see the proud citizens of Rome gazing with their cruel eyes into the vast arena below. A softer spirit has conquered Caesar and pagan Rome. But there is as much enmity against God as ever. Now it finds a less public arena, and a meaner mode of torture. Today, the tried one suffers alone and misses the encouragement of Christian eyes. At times one feels that it were better for him to fight with beasts at Ephesus than to bear the taunts, threats, and slanders of ungodly family members. Have faith in God in your hidden sorrow! Cry to Him in the secret of your soul, and you will bear your load. Of your secret martyrdom, angels will be spectators, and Christ will suffer in you. Fear not. Out of weakness you shall be made strong by faith.

We have others who have to stand against *assaults of unbelief.* Skepticism, biblical criticism, and even a vile blasphemy breaks out against believers. Do they really expect that we are to answer on the spur of the moment every objection that they raise? Do not try to answer cavillers, but if you do, make sure that faith is your weapon. If you take the wooden sword of your own reasoning, you may easily be beaten. Believe for yourself, because God has said it. Fix in your mind: "This is God's Book. This is His infallible revelation, and I believe it against every argument that can possibly be urged against it. Let God be true, but every man a liar." This will be sure defensive ground, but if you get off that rock, you will soon find yourself sinking and staggering. For an offensive weapon, take "the sword of the Spirit, which is the word of God" (Eph. 6:17). If this does not serve your turn, nothing will. Have a thorough and childlike faith in the revelation of the Most High. You will be made strong in those mental conflicts for which in yourself you are so weak.

I may also be writing to those who suffer under *mental depression.* Some of us are by constitution inclined to that condition. I have sometimes envied those good people who are never excited with joy, and consequently are seldom or never despondent. At the same time, when I rise as upon eagles' wings in joyous rapture, I feel very glad to be capable of the blissful excitement. Yet if you soar to the skies, you are very apt to drop below the sea level. He who can fly, can faint. Elijah, after he had slain the prophets of Baal, was found fleeing into the wilderness from the face of Jezebel (1 Kings 19:3). If you happen to have been born on a foggy day and to have swallowed so much of that fog that you have found it shading your spirit many a time ever since, you can be strong only by faith. If you seldom can call yourself joyful, the only cure for depression is faith. Settle this in your heart: "Whether I am up or down, the Lord Jesus Christ is the same. Whether I sing or sigh, the promise is true, and the Promiser is faithful. Whether I stand on the summit or am hidden in the vale, the covenant stands fast and everlasting love abides." Believe in Christ, though you see no flashes of delight or sparkles of joy. We are safe in Jesus. If you will stand firm in Him, you will be made strong.

It may even be that you are called to suffer in your mind *for the sake of others.* Some years ago I preached a sermon from the text, "My God, My God, why hast thou forsaken me?," and in a mournful degree I felt what I preached as my own cry. I felt an agony of spirit, for I was under an awful sense of being forsaken of God and could not understand why I was surrounded by such thick darkness. Yet I could discover no sin in my life to bring such suffering. When I went back into the vestry, there was an elderly man in a horror of great darkness who said to me, "I have never met with any person who has been where I am. I trust there is hope for me." Afterwards I conducted him from the verge of insanity into the open, healthy place of peace through believing. I fear that I would never have touched his case if I had not been in the miry clay myself. When this occurs, we must have faith in God. If you are chosen to be a leader and a helper, be satisfied to endure hardness with the full belief that it is all right and that God not only will bring you through but also will bless somebody else by the means of your tribulations.

Nothing but faith in the grand old doctrines of grace and in the ever-living and unchanging God can bring back the church again to the full tide of blessing, making her to be the deliverer of the nations for Christ. And nothing but faith in the Lord Jesus can save you or me.

Love grows out of faith yet more by the discoveries of beauty in Christ that faith is sure to make. Faith is the soul's eye and telescope by which it sees that which is so far off as to be otherwise invisible. Holy faith gazes upon the character of the Lord Jesus, realizes His person, and discerns His matchless work, and so creates the knowledge out of which comes love. Faith stands like the cherubim upon the golden mercy seat, looking downward always upon the blood sprinkled propitiatory, admiring and wondering, spying out something new every hour, and thus filling itself with ever-increased delight with those things that the angels desire to look into. Out of this gracious discernment comes admiring love. Faith delights to unveil the superlative beauties of the Beloved before the gaze of love, and then faith and love unite in crying out, "Yes. He is altogether lovely." Those who believe can say, "We see Jesus," and those whose hearts are won by Him can add, "We love him because He first loved us."

Chapter Eight

Faith Working by Love

For in Jesus Christ neither circumcision availeth any thing, nor uncircumcision; but faith which worketh by love—Galatians 5:6.

ALL THE WAYS OF JUSTIFICATION by human works and outward forms are set aside by the Apostle Paul. In one sentence he closes up every road that is cast up by man and opens up the way of the Lord, even the way of salvation by grace through faith in Jesus Christ. Some hope to be saved by ritualism only to be struck down by this word: "Neither circumcision availeth any thing." Others who place their reliance upon a sort of antiritualism are smitten by "nor uncircumcision." As the Jews relied upon circumcision, so do many depend upon baptism and sacraments. Paul's word has not changed. Others glory in the uncircumcision of practicing no ceremonies and a disorderly worship that tends to make them feel righteous. It is as easy to make a self-righteousness out of the plainness of the Quaker as out of the gaudiness of the Catholic. One confidence is as fatal as the other. We may glory in the simplicity of our worship and the scripturalness of our baptism, but if we think that outward things will save us because they are scripturally simple, we shall err as much as they do who multiply pompous processions and gorgeous services.

The outward, whether decorated or unadorned, whether fixed

or free, touches not the saving thing. The only thing that can save us is faith in Jesus Christ. Faith brings us in contact with the healing fountain, and so our natural disease of sin is removed. It appropriates in our behalf the result of the Redeemer's service and sacrifice, and so we become accepted in Him. Anything short of this must fail. It is the rending of the garment while the heart is unbroken, the washing of the outside of the cup while the inner part is very filthy.

The apostle distinguishes between faith itself and its many imitations. True faith will save a man though it is but as a grain of mustard seed, but then it must be the genuine silver and not a mere plated article. Real faith will save us, but forgeries of it will increase our peril. Assurance is of God, but presumption is of the devil. The test of true faith is that it works: "*faith which worketh.*" To that end it must first of all be alive, for it is clear that a dead faith cannot work. There must be heart in our faith, and the Spirit of God breathing in it, or it will not be the living faith of a living child of God. "Wherefore by their fruits ye shall know them" (Matt. 7:20) is one of Christ's own rules for testing men and things, and we are to know faith by that which comes of it—by what it does for us and in us and through us. Faith is not worth having if it is fruitless.

A further distinction is also set forth, namely, that true faith "worketh *by love.*" There are some who do many works as the result of a kind of faith who, nevertheless, are not justified. King Herod, for instance, feared the stern language of John the Baptist and the judgments that would come upon him if he rejected the second Elijah's warnings, but his faith worked through fear, and he murdered his minister. The great test of the working of saving faith is this: it "worketh by love." If you are led by your faith in Jesus Christ to love and serve Him, you have real faith.

How vital the connection that exists between faith and love! As we look into the intermingling and intertwisting of the roots and branches of love and faith, may we also glimpse what state our soul is in.

Faith Always Produces Love

"Faith which worketh by love." When faith has anything to do, she walks to the field with love at her side. The two graces are inseparable. Like Mary and Martha, they are sisters living in the same house. Faith, like Mary, sits at Jesus' feet and hears His words, and then love diligently goes about the house and rejoices to honor the divine Lord. Faith is light, while love is heat, and in every beam of grace from the Sun of righteousness you will find a measure of each. True faith in God cannot exist without love to Him, nor sincere love without faith.

This happens *by a necessity of faith's own nature.* The moment a man believes in Jesus Christ, he loves Him as a matter of course. To trust the bleeding Lamb and not love Him is a thing not to be imagined. Faith is a gold ring that in every case the heavenly jeweller sets with the beryl of love. Water faith with a drop of God's own dew and it blossoms with love. The first steps of the soul when it begins to believe in God are desires after Him in which there is a measure of love. Look back at the first day when you saw the Lord by faith. Did you not love Him immediately? Aye! We sometimes fear we loved Him better then than now, though I hope that is not the case. Faith creates love as summer breeds flowers. Our first love came with our first faith by a necessity of nature that can never change.

Love grows out of faith yet more *by the discoveries of beauty in Christ that faith is sure to make.* Faith is the soul's eye and telescope by which it sees that which is so far off as to be otherwise invisible. Holy faith gazes upon the character of the Lord Jesus, realizes His person, and discerns His matchless work, and so creates the knowledge out of which comes love. Faith stands like the cherubim upon the golden mercy seat, looking downward always upon the blood sprinkled propitiatory, admiring and wondering, spying out something new every hour, and thus filling itself with ever-increased delight with those things that the angels desire to look into. Out of this gracious discernment comes admiring love. Faith delights to unveil the superlative beauties of the Beloved before the gaze of love, and then faith and love unite in crying out, "Yes. He is altogether lovely." Those who believe can say, "We see Jesus," and those whose hearts are won by Him can add, "We love him because He first loved us."

Faith creates love next *by its appropriation of that which it discerns,* for while faith is the soul's eye, it is also the mind's hand by which it grasps the blessing. Faith sees the love of Christ and says, "He loved me and gave himself for me" (Gal. 2:20). Faith sees the wounds of Jesus and perceives His deity through those windows of ruby and cries out, "My Lord and my God" (John 20:28). Love is sure to arise out of a sense of possession. Does not a mother love her child very much because it is her own? It was this sense of belonging that made the psalmist sing, "O God, thou art my God; early will I seek thee" (Ps. 63:1). Even things like silver and gold, possessions and land, when they are a person's own, are apt to be loved for the affections to that which is possessed: "For where your treasure is, there will your heart be also" (Matt. 6:21). Hence the danger that comes when worldly things hold the heart captive from mounting upward toward God. This is true with Christ. If Christ is yours by faith, love cries out, "This is my beloved and this is my friend." Love rejoices in Jesus as her possession, triumphs in Him, and sweetly sings of love to Him.

Faith further stimulates love *by its enjoying the mercy and then leading the heart to a grateful acknowledgment of the source of the mercy.* There are two links in the chain in this case: faith wins the mercy in prayer, the mercy is enjoyed, and then out of the enjoyment springs love to Him who gave it. What innumerable gifts faith has already brought us. It is as though a key has been given to God's storeroom and we are allowed to feast upon all that the Lord has prepared for them that love him. To know the privilege of heirship with Christ, does not this bind you fast to your Elder Brother? I hope that you keep your eyes open to see the everyday providential mercies you receive. Spiritual blessings are coming to you from the God of all grace, filling you with joy unspeakable and cementing your soul to your Redeemer. Unless your heart is altogether out of order, you love God better and better because He is manifesting His love to you more and more. Is it not so?

It does this even more sweetly *by the familiarity with God that it creates in the heart,* for faith is in the habit of going to God with all her burdens and coming away with her load removed. Faith has the daily practice of pleading promises with God, speaking to Him face to face as a man speaks to his friend, and receiving favors from the right hand of the Most High that make even her expectant soul to wonder. Faith commences with God in the morning as Abraham did and walks with him in the field at evening as Isaac did. Faith's life is in God even as the life of a fish is in the sea. The bosom of

Jesus Christ is the pillow of faith, and the heart of God is the pavilion of faith. Because faith keeps us so near to God, it causes us to love Him. The pilgrims of Emmaus said, "Did not our heart burn within us, while he talked with us by the way, and while he opened to us the scriptures?" (Luke 24:32). Those who know His love must feel His spell upon their affections, holding them captive. There is none like Him among the sons of men. His beauties ravish the heart. If Jesus should lift the veil and let us glimpse Him for a moment, our hearts would melt within us.

This familiarity with Christ soon gives birth to congeniality of disposition and spirit, for those who are much with Christ become much like Christ. A mirror upon which the sun is shining is bright itself, flashing its reflected rays afar. He who walks with wise men will be wise, but he who dwells with the infinite wisdom shall be taught by God. Happy couples who live together in love become very much like each other, sharing the same aims and values. So do the saint and the Savior grow together, only the growth is all on one side: we "grow up into him in all things, which is the head, even Christ" (Eph. 4:15). Love is nurtured in the soul by a growing likeness of disposition. Wherever there is congeniality of taste and mind and view and disposition and spirit, love becomes strong and well established. Thus faith, by begetting in us likeness to Christ, causes love for Christ to become a mighty power in the soul.

Surely all these points sufficiently show that faith creates love in the soul wherever it really dwells. But do not begin to say, "I am afraid I do not love Jesus as I should." Take it for granted that you do not love Him to the full of His infinite worth, and instead of raising questions about the degree of your love, ask yourself whether you believe in Him. Are you trusting in the Lord Jesus? Are you confiding in Him? Because if the root is there, the flower will soon appear. Do not talk of trying to love God. You cannot force yourself to love anyone. Love cannot be bought or forced. It must be free-born. Love is a mysterious something not to be described by the cold maker of definitions, but it is always a product of something else that goes before it. If you believe, you will love; if you do not believe, you will never love till you do believe. If you trust Jesus, love may slumber in you like fire in smoldering wood, but before long it will burn vehemently. Look well to your faith and your love will not fail.

Love Is Entirely Dependent Upon Faith

"Faith which worketh by love." Love does not work of itself, except in the strength of faith. Love is so dependent on faith that *it cannot exist without it*. No man loves a Savior in whom he puts no confidence. There may be an admiration for the character of Christ, but the emotion that the Scriptures treat as "love" comes into the heart only when we trust Christ.

Certainly *love cannot flourish except as faith flourishes*. If you fall into troubled times and doubt the Lord's wisdom or goodness in sending it, the next thing will be that your heart will be cold toward Him and you will quarrel with Him. The two graces must diminish or increase together. If you attain a simple, childlike confidence that rests in Christ as a babe on its mother's bosom, your love shall be made perfect. When we want to trust ourselves a little and fail to rest in God's goodness, you have to ask yourself whether you love Him or not. May God the Holy Spirit work in us a mighty strength of faith that we may have a love as strong as death, immortal as divinity.

As love cannot flourish without faith, so *it cannot work without it*. Love is a great designer and planner, but faith shows the way. Love sits down and says, "May the world be converted to Christ," but faith goes out and preaches the gospel. Love cries, "I would to God that the children knew Jesus," but faith opens the Sunday school and teaches the children. Love must have faith to give it muscle, sinew, and strength; therefore, take good care of your faith.

Love is as Solomon's lily, dropping sweet-smelling myrrh. How fair to look upon! But the lovely flower is joined by its stalk to a living root that is hidden underground. Faith is the bulb out of which love comes as the perfection of beauty. Love for God, if it is to be worthy of the name, must be soundly rooted in Jesus. It cannot abide without it but is carried away by wind and flood, like the house built on the sand. Too often we see the appearance of ardent affection for Jesus that is without knowledge and humility, without penitance and childlike faith, and we tremble to hear them sing, "Oh, yes, I do love Jesus." We fear lest the building that rises up in a night should vanish like the soap bubble of a child which, though it is adorned with all the colors of the rainbow, dissolves in an instant. See that you are rooted and grounded in the knowledge of Christ and genuine faith in Him, lest the high tower of professed love should soon lie in ruins and indifference.

Faith Displays Its Power by Love

"Faith which worketh by love." Faith is like a blacksmith, strong and vigorous, who has love for *his arms*. Faith lifts not a finger without love. Faith believes and resolves, and then it proceeds to action, but the power with which it can work lies in love. Faith without love would be a person without arms. More than this: it is not only faith's arms but *his tools*. Love is faith's hammer and file and anvil. Love can be fitted for every task of faith, however large or small. Love is just a tool, for love will teach a little child or evangelize a nation. Love can stand and burn at the stake, or it can drop two pennies into the offering box. Love hopes all things and endures all thing. It is a wonderfully handy tool of sacred grace that faith has adopted to work with. It can strike and it can cut, it is good at uniting and good for breaking, and it will avail for anything that faith wishes to perform. Only let faith wield love as its instrument and it can fashion whatever divine wisdom tells it to form.

Love is also faith's *furnace*. All the tools in the world will not suffice the smith unless he can blow the coals and create a fervent heat. What is there that can kindle the heat of enthusiasm like a sincere love for God? Faith believes God and rejoices in Him; then loves comes, and the heart grows hot as Nebuchadnezzar's furnace. What is there that cannot be performed if we have love enough? This is the great fire that burns in human hearts when God the Holy Spirit sheds abroad the love of Jesus there (Rom. 5:5). This fire will yet consume all sin and melt all hardness. None can quench it. Everything must yield before it. Faith blows on the coals of love, and tasks that were as hard as iron become easily workable when plunged into its glowing flame.

When all is melted and ready to flow, love is faith's *mold*. Faith pours out all it does into the mold of God's love, fashioning its works according to the divine pattern of love in Christ Jesus. As Jesus loved us, even so would we love one another. As Christ loved the Father and glorified the Father by fulfilling the law and making Himself a sacrifice, even so are we willing to lay down our lives for the brethren and for the Father's honor.

What is more, love is faith's *metal*, for into the mold of love faith pours love itself. Love is the substance of every good work. Melt it down in the fining pot, and holiness is love. If there is any virtue, zeal, consecration, or holy daring, its substance is love. All the grand deeds that the heroes of the cross have performed are composed of the solid metal of love to Jesus Christ. Be it great or be it little, he who has served God has always brought into the sanctuary an offering of pure love comparable to the gold of Ophir.

Love is also faith's *burnisher and file*, and with it she finishes all her work very carefully. Have you never lovingly gone over all your work to give it the finishing touches? It is the same when we look over our lives. I have often said, "That will not do, for I see self there. Oh, there is unbelief again. There is too much of self-will over there." And with tearful love I have filed down and polished my poor efforts and found love to be an excellent burnisher.

Thus faith works by love. If you are working for God in any other way than this, you will make a mess of it. The law can never help you to such work as God accepts. The law is fitted to produce bars for a prison but not pillars for a temple. You must work for God because you love Him. No other labor can be acceptable to Him. Duty must be turned into delight. Weariness must be turned to joy. We may discover our service is not gold but gilded dross. Take it away! This is forced service devoid of the lifeblood of obedience like fruit without flavor or scent. That which is done because a man loves God, however humble the service may be, is accepted by God. True affection to Him who redeemed you never fails to present an acceptable tribute before the living God.

Love Perfects Faith

While love owes everything to faith, faith eventually becomes a debtor to love. Love *leads the soul into admiration* and so increases faith. Love that has the dove's eyes to see everything fair spies out more and more of Christ's perfections, and thus she aids the eye of faith. Love sees more of the Lord's power and faithfulness and immutability, and faith at once concludes, "I can trust Him more than ever."

Love *forbids unbelief* and so helps faith, for love says, "How can we grieve Him by doubts?" To love forbids distrust. The lack of trust in married life is the death of love, but love is instinctively tender of showing anything like suspicion toward a spouse. Love believes all things, endures all thing, and will not tolerate mistrust that it knows to be a worm at the very core of the heart. Love for Christ forbids doubt and kills the foxes of distrust that spoil the tender vines of faith.

Love for Jesus feels that it is better to distrust all men and angels than doubt the dear Redeemer who poured out His blood to prove His love. Distrust the heavens, for they shall pass away. Distrust the earth, for it shall be utterly burned up. Distrust man, for he is as a broken reed. But never distrust God. Lean on Him with your whole weight and undivided confidence. So love teaches, and faith learns her lesson.

Moreover, *perfect love casts out fear* because fear has torment (1 John 4:18). And when perfect love casts out fear, faith has room to display its strength. Love has not learned to be afraid, nor will she permit the work of faith to become a labor of a trembling slave. Dread! Where can that find a lodging in the heart that loves? The love of the child for the parent is without dread. Love gives boldness and yet is most reverent. Chilliness and coldness are not for the children of God. They are called to close relationship with their heavenly Father, and the meeting place is not at Sinai but at Calvary. Faith and love dwell in the house of the Lord forever. This is the joy of love, that it brings us into such a close personal relationship with God in Jesus Christ. All slavish fear is gone. Trust your God with everything. Trust Him in little things, trust Him in great things, trust Him in your joys, trust Him in your sorrows. This love is an eminent grace.

Faith works. Let us work because we have faith. I wish that every member of Christ's church were at work for Him. Faith that does not work gives way to factions and quarrels. May our good Lord spare us from such a calamity. Love one another much, and love Christ more, and love the souls of perishing sinners. Yes, love them so that you will not let them perish if you can do anything toward their salvation. Personal doing of good is needed if love is to be real. The love of Jesus made Him seek and save the lost, and if ours is worth the name we shall be engaged in the same holy work.

But to work in love, we must believe. Go to prayer and renew your faith in Jesus. May the Holy Spirit lead you afresh to the dying love of Jesus. I often go straight back to the cross from where I started when I set out for heaven. I say, "I rest on Jesus only." Abide in Him evermore. Let Him be everything to you. Constant faith will create fervent love, and fervent love will do persevering work. So we shall be a people zealous for good works.

*T*rust Jesus Christ alone to utterly save you. Sink or swim, throw yourself into the sea of Jesus' love. You shall see the glory of God in your pardon, in your new creation, in your being sustained under temptation, in your being kept in the hours of life and in the night of death, in your being lifted up at the day of judgment to receive an acquittal and being pronounced faultless before His presence with exceeding great joy (Jude 24)! I have known myself as defiled, corrupt, unworthy, but I see the day coming when I shall be wearing a crown, waving a palm branch, bowing before the eternal throne, having neither spot nor wrinkle, nor any such thing. My soul has leapt at the very thought that I shall tread the streets of gold, passing through the gates of pearl, and see His face, and bow before Him! I, who was once filled with sin and corruption, filled to the brim with the vision of God. You and I will meet there, and what a wonder it will be that we should have ever gotten there! It is no wonder that in heaven they strike up that grand old song that will always be new: "Unto him that loved us, and washed us from our sins in his own blood, And hath made us kings and priests unto God and his Father; to him be glory and dominion for ever and ever" (Rev. 1:5–6). I am of the same mind as the good old soul who said that if Jesus Christ ever took her to heaven, He would never hear the last of it. And He never shall!

Chapter Nine

Faith Seeing God's Glory

Jesus saith unto her, Said I not unto thee, that, if thou wouldest believe, thou shouldest see the glory of God?—John 11:40.

IT IS NOT EVERY MAN whose actions match his words, but of the Son of Man, Christ Jesus, it may be said that whatever His lips have promised, His hands perform. He can, after the fact has transpired, turn to His disciples and say, "Is it not just as I spoke?" Christ has said that those who believe in Him will have peace, and He will never turn away from that word. If you cast your cares upon Him, you shall have peace and happiness evermore. There is no promise that Christ has made that He is not prepared to keep. There is no blessing that He presents to the hand of our faith that is either unreal, a sham, or a mockery. You shall find that Christ's gold is not mere tinsel but is true, and that His silver is silver tried in the furnace—excellent spending money, both for time and eternity.

Jesus said that through our faith we see the glory of God. I would like to show how faith does this practically—first, how faith works as regards *the care we have for others' souls,* and second, how faith works in regard *to our own soul.*

Faith and the Care for Others' Souls

Those who have personally tasted and known the sweetness of true Christianity are not selfishly satisfied merely to rejoice in their religion but long that others, too, may taste and see that the Lord is good (Ps. 34:8). But a sincere desire to bring others to Christ will often be met with *cases that stagger your faith*, throwing you back entirely upon your God and compelling you to make your passionate appeal to His omnipotence. It seems to me that our text addresses itself specially to those who meet with such cases.

Poor Martha, when she saw the stone rolled away from the tomb of her dead brother Lazarus, was shocked with what would meet the eye and nostrils of her Lord, and so, in deep concern and almost alarm, she declared, "Lord, by this time he stinketh" (John 11:39). The sight was too revolting, for he had been dead nearly four days and a terrible havoc already would have been worked upon his body. Martha could not bear that the Savior be exposed to such a spectacle. Now, how often do we meet with men and women, young and old, whose case is a very terrible one. We prefer to not talk about it. It involves getting among the putrid things, for "it is a shame even to speak of those things which are done of them in secret" (Eph. 5:12). We come upon lives that are shocking, terrible, fearful. We may desire that a stone might cover the cave so we do not have to see what's there, that they may be left unobserved as cases too vile for the ordinary gazer to look upon. Immorality, debauchery, dishonesty, and everything that is dreadful fill the lives of people. We are tempted to think that the gospel is out of place there and the publishing of the news of pardoning love will be like throwing pearls before swine.

Others reach out to those who seem hopelessly lost through a hardness of heart. There are those who do not want to hear the gospel that once greatly moved them: they have grown tired of it. There is the daughter whose refuses her mother's concerns and plunges into sin and excess. There is the son who refuses to heed his father's counsel and pleadings. There are those who walk away from Christianity and actually deny the faith, declaring it a sham. Perhaps blasphemy has taken the place of an attentive ear to the Word. You feel as you think about this one who is the object of your love that you would give up your very heart if you could but have hope of his salvation, but he seems to have gone too far. The one whom you have been pleading for night and day plunges deeper and deeper into sin, turning your home into a bitter place of hard endurance. To you, Christ says, "Said I not unto thee, that, if thou wouldest believe, thou shouldest see the glory of God?" The death of Lazarus, the burial, the stinking—all of this is only a platform for the divine glory to display itself upon. This horrible sin, the hardness of heart, the rejection of the Word—all of this is only a stage where the grace of God, in answer to your prayerful faith, shall come and do its wonders.

Be encouraged of what you will yet see if your faith is able to lay hold upon Christ. You will see *the conversion of the lost one,* and then you will see the glory of God, for you will say, "Only God could have given His only begotten Son for such a sinner as this!" Did it never strike you as strange that there should be two—one, the perfectly holy Christ, the beloved Son of God; and, on the other hand, a reeling, cursing, blaspheming drunkard—and that God would sooner smite His Son than smite the drunkard? That God should bring His Son to grief and suffering rather than the blasphemer? Truly, when the Jews made the choice of the robber Barabbas rather than Christ, it was a strange choice, and only to be understood by their wicked infatuation. But here, such is the power of God's love that when one out of two must suffer, He chooses that the innocent Christ should die and the sinner go free! Truly "God commendeth his love toward us, in that, while we were yet sinners, Christ died for us" (Rom. 5:8).

Is it not marvelous that Jesus Christ could really give Himself for even the greatest sinner who troubles our lives? It is the wonder of wonders as the Apostle Paul notes: "For scarcely for a righteous man will one die: yet peradventure for a good man some would even dare to die" (Rom. 5:7). What! Did Christ shed His blood for thieves and harlots and drunkards? Yes, indeed, as much as for the self-righteous, and even more so, for while the self-righteous miss heaven by reason of their pride and refusal of grace, some of these vile ones, coming humbly to the Cross, find pardon through the precious blood.

We truly *do* see the glory of God when such a soul is converted. We cannot comprehend the miracle of love it expresses when a soul so spiritually corrupted is helped by sovereign grace to trust in Christ. As the glory of Christ's power was seen in Lazarus' coming out of the grave, despite the corruption of four days' death, so the same glory is seen in the conversion of every sinner.

I have seen the most foul-mouthed person come to Christ and pray better and much more earnestly than half of the other church members. The depth of feeling, the groanings that cannot be uttered, come welling up from his grateful, adoring heart. Does "the woman in the city, which was a sinner" love the Savior (Luke 7:37)? Yes, and she washes His feet with her tears and wipes them with the hair of her head, doing more for Christ than Simon did, whose guest He was, though Simon thought he had done so much. Grace can make bright saints out of the darkest sinner, taking the very scum of Satan's dominions and making them into sparkling jewels to glitter in the crown of divine grace forever. Whether in your own life or in the life of another, never let the devil tell you that Christ cannot save. Look at Lazarus and see how life can come back at the Savior's word. The glory of God is seen in the conversion of the sinner, but most conspicuously in the conversion of the chief of sinners.

And this glory is also seen in the fact that these sinners, when saved, hold on and continue to the end. The glory of God and the power of the gospel are remarkably displayed when we see that they do not go back to their old sins. They become such new creations that it is impossible for them to return to their old lifestyle and its evil loves and desires. Never stop praying for those whose condition staggers your faith. We should only hear the Savior say that He is making a larger room for the display of His matchless grace. Such cases are never hopeless.

But who is it that sees the glory of God in the conversion of a soul? When an artist produces a masterpiece, he likes others to see it. And such is the case with God's work in a person's soul. When a sinner is saved, all eyes behold it. *The man's neighbors see it.* Some of them hate the change, but they cannot help seeing it. His wife and children know it. His relatives and friends wonder aloud at it. They may jeer at it, but they must say, "What is this? Here is a faith that really has power to alter a life, taking them out of the old ruts of sin and putting them on a new highway that turns their minds in another direction."

Enemies see the conversion, too, and, what is still more remarkable, it becomes a theme of *wonder in other worlds*! Devils see it, and they do not like it. They resolve to overthrow the man, but all the devils in hell cannot destroy a child of God. You may be familiar with Toplady's saying about the grace of God. He says it is like leaven: if you once get it into the cake, you can boil it, you can fry it, you can bake it, but you cannot get it out. Such is the case with the grace of God in a man's heart. God does what the devil cannot undo when He makes "a new creature" (2 Cor. 5:17). And then the angels see it. We have God's Word for that, for we are told that "there is joy in the presence of the angels of God over one sinner that repenteth" (Luke 15:10). When a soul finds the Savior, it affects three worlds in one moment. The earth is made glad, hell howls with indignation, and heaven is set ablaze in extraordinary joy. Do not the harps of the angels thrill with super-celestial harmonies when they hear of sinners being saved! Do they not lift up a new song and yet more exalted praise to Him who trod the winepress alone and whose victory these souls are the reward!

Yes, earth and heaven and hell, all know of it. *We know it* for the text says, "Said I not unto thee, that, if thou wouldest believe, thou shouldest see the glory of God?" We should labor on to win the lost, though we cannot yet see it, but it is a great delight to be privileged to see the sheaves cut and then carry them to the Great Husbandman and say, "That is a sheaf you have given me." What an encouragement to continue in God's service when people are converted!

So why is it that we are not more successful? Let us heed that Jesus said, "If thou wouldest believe." God blesses in a very great measure according to what we believe will be the result. We should always preach and pray in faith that God will save souls because He loves them. God is the "rewarder of them that diligently seek him" (Heb. 11:6) and has promised that His Word will not return to Him void but will prosper in the thing whereto He has sent it (Isa. 55:11). We should always be expecting conversions.

Expect the blessing of God. It is coming! It is coming! God is blessing His church, and He intends to bless it yet more. He has opened the windows of heaven, and He is pouring out the blessing, so that we will not have room enough to receive it. Only let us pray and work, and God will bless us, and the ends of the earth will fear

Him. The heart of the matter is that we believe. Mother, can you believe for your child? Husband, can you believe about your wife? May God help you to believe Him! Depend upon it that the struggle is there. It is much harder for you to believe in God than it is for God to convert your wife, much harder for you to trust God about your child than it is for Him to save your child. When we can believe in Him, and, believing, boldly pray for it and expect it, we shall get it. And that person who was so repulsive yesterday shall be fragrant with divine grace tomorrow. He who was rotting in his tomb the other day, so far gone that men turned away from him, shall come into Christ's church and be found among the living in Zion, making the church on earth and in heaven glad in his presence.

Faith Working in Our Own Lives

Perhaps you once thought yourself to be very good, but the Holy Spirit has met with you and caused you to see yourself. Now you are ashamed of yourself. You feel as if you are dead, as if you have no power, no life.

Like Lazarus, you actually feel buried. Satan has told you that there is no hope for someone who is as corrupt in soul as you are. You cannot sleep at night or hardly endure yourself during the day. Your fears that God will leave you buried out of His sight seem to prove true. Turn your thoughts to the truth: God thinks well of you and wants to bless you. You may say that you have no feeling, no emotions, that you cannot repent, and a great many other things. But, can you believe that Christ can save you? Can you trust Him to do it? If you can, then all there is of hardness and evil—even if it were ten times more—could not avail to keep you out of heaven. "Though your sins be as scarlet, they shall be as white as snow; though they be red like crimson, they shall be as wool" (Isa. 1:18). Pardoning love can melt the hardest of hearts. Christ is exalted on high to give you repentance. He can take your stubbornness and make you willing in the day of His power.

Have you not heard the story? It was God Himself who died on Calvary. It was none other than that same one who made the heavens, who came down to earth and became a man for the sake of men and on the bloody tree died in agonies extreme. He, "very God of very God," though a man like you, died that sin might be put away and sinners be saved. Can you believe this? If you will believe on Him, you shall see the glory of God. "But I cannot see," you say. No! No! No! It does not say if you can see, but if you believe, you shall see. Believing comes first, and then follows the seeing, and what is it you are to see? The glory of God. In the teeth of your soul's corruption and in defiance of all the powers of evil, God's glory will make it impossible for a single note of praise to be given to you, but all the glory shall be to His rich, all-conquering, sovereign grace.

Trust Jesus Christ alone to utterly save you. Sink or swim, throw yourself into the sea of Jesus' love. You shall see the glory of God in your pardon, in your new creation, in your being sustained under temptation, in your being kept in the hours of life and in the night of death, in your being lifted up at the day of judgment to receive an acquittal and being pronounced faultless before His presence with exceeding great joy (Jude 24)! I have known myself as defiled, corrupt, unworthy, but I see the day coming when I shall be wearing a crown, waving a palm branch, bowing before the eternal throne, having neither spot nor wrinkle, nor any such thing. My soul has leapt at the very thought that I shall tread the streets of gold, passing through the gates of pearl, and see *His* face, and bow before *Him*! I, who was once filled with sin and corruption, filled to the brim with the vision of God. You and I will meet there, and what a wonder it will be that we should have ever gotten there! It is no wonder that in heaven they strike up that grand old song that will always be new: "Unto him that loved us, and washed us from our sins in his own blood, And hath made us kings and priests unto God and his Father; to him be glory and dominion for ever and ever" (Rev. 1:5–6). I am of the same mind as the good old soul who said that if Jesus Christ ever took her to heaven, He would never hear the last of it. And He never shall!

Come forth from the grave! Come forth! Jesus calls you to come and trust Him! Not only will He make you a new creature, but He promises to take you one day to where the angels dwell, above all, where He dwells. He is the Blessed One, whom, though we have not seen, we love and unceasingly adore. He calls you to be in His bosom forever, to be kissed with the kisses of His mouth, to be His dear one, to live in His Father's house where the many mansions are! What a glorious sight that will be! It is all yours in Christ Jesus. May God help you to believe.

*P*ersons who are born again really do overcome the world. How is this brought about? The text says, "This is the victory that overcometh the world, even our faith." Christians do not triumph over the world by reason. Reason is a very good thing, and no one should find fault with it. Reason is a candle, but faith is the sun. While I prefer the sun, I do not put out the candle. I use my reason constantly, but when I come to real warfare, reason is a wooden sword. It breaks, it snaps, while faith, that sword of true Jerusalem metal, cuts to the dividing of soul and body. Those who do something significant in the world are always men of faith. The person who wins the battle is the one who knows he will win and vows to be the victor. Those who never get on in this world are those who are always afraid to do a thing for fear they cannot accomplish it. Who climbs to the top of the Alps? The person who says, "I will do it, or I will die." Let such a person make up his mind that he can do a thing, and he will do it if it is within the range of possibility. Those who have lifted the standard and, grasping it with a firm hand, have held it up in the midst of stormy strife and battle are the men of faith. Men of fear and trembling run, but men of faith, whose boldness is etched on their foreheads like brass, lift their eyes "unto the hills, from whence cometh my help" (Ps. 121:1), believing in God.

Chapter Ten

The Victory of Faith

*For whatsoever is born of God overcometh the world: and this is the victory that overcometh the world, even our faith—*1 John 5:4.

THE EPISTLES OF JOHN are perfumed with love. The word occurs continually, while the Spirit enters into every sentence. Each letter is thoroughly soaked and impregnated with this heavenly honey. If John speaks of God, His name must be love. When the brethren are mentioned, John loves them. Even of the world itself, John writes, "For God so loved the world, that he gave his only begotten Son" (John 3:16). From the opening to the conclusion, love is the manner, the motive, the substance, and the aim.

It is astonishing, therefore, to hear a sound of war in so peaceful a writing as John's. It is not the voice of love, surely, that says, "He that is born of God overcometh the world." Here are martial words of strife and contention, agony and wrestling, so unlike the love whose words are softer than butter and whose utterances flow more easily than oil. Love has no harsh words within its lips, only velvet lines its mouth. Here we have warfare, strife until death, battle throughout life, fighting with a certainty of victory. How is it that the same gospel that always speaks peace here proclaims a warfare?

How can it be? Simply because there is something in the world that is antagonistic to love. There are principles around us that cannot bear the gospel light, and, therefore, before light can come, it must chase the darkness. Before summer reigns, it must battle with old winter and send it howling away in the winds of March, shedding its tears in April showers. So also, before any great or good thing can have the mastery of this world, it must do battle with it. Satan has seated himself on his blood-stained throne, and who shall get him down without a fight? As darkness broods over the nations, so the sun cannot establish his empire of light until he has pierced night with the arrowy sunbeams and made it flee away.

We also read that Christ came not to send peace on earth, but a sword: "The father shall be divided against the son, and the son against the father; the mother against the daughter, and the daughter against the mother" (Luke 12:53). This occurs not intentionally but as a means to an end, because there must always be a struggle before truth and righteousness can reign. Alas, for the earth is the battlefield where good must combat with evil. Angels look on and hold their breath, burning with a desire to mingle in the conflict. But the troops of the Captain of Salvation may only be soldiers of the cross, and that slender band must fight alone and yet shall triumph gloriously. They shall be enough for the conquest, and the motto of their standard is *Enough*. Enough by the arm of the helping Trinity.

The Apostle John describes three key points regarding our warfare in the text. First, he speaks of a *great victory*: "this is the victory." Second, he mentions a *great birth*: "whatsoever is born of God." And third, he extols a *great grace*, whereby we overcome the world, "even our faith."

A Great Victory

The text speaks of the greatest victory of victories. There have been great battles where nations met in strife and one nation has overcome the other. But who has read of a victory that overcame the world? Some will say that Alexander the Great conquered the world, but I answer no. He was himself the vanquished man, even when he seemed to possess all things. He fought for the world and won, but then note how the world mastered its master, conquering and lashing the monarch who had been its scourge. See the royal youth weeping and stretching out his hands with idiotic cries for another world that he might ravage. Outwardly Alexander seemed to overcome old earth, but in reality, within his inmost soul, the world had conquered him. The earth overwhelmed him, wrapped him in the dream of ambition, clothed him with the chains of covetousness, so that when he had everything, he was still not satisfied. Like a poor slave, Alexander was dragged on at the chariot wheels of the world, crying, moaning, lamenting, because he could not win another.

Who is the man who ever overcame the world? Let him stand forward. He is a Triton among the minnows; he shall outshine Caesar; he shall outmatch Wellington, if he can say he has overcome the world. It is so rare a thing, a victory so prodigious, a conquest so tremendous, that he who can claim to have won it may walk among his fellows like Saul, with head and shoulders far above them. This person shall command our respect; his very presence shall awe us into reverence; his speech shall persuade us to obedience; and yielding honor to whom honor is due, we'll say when we listen to his voice, " 'Tis even as if an angel shook his wings."

For the Christian to overcome the world is a tough battle, I warrant you. It is not one that carpet knights might win, who dash to battle on some sunshiny day, look at the host, then turn their horses around and daintily dismount at the door of their silken tents. It is not a victory for a new recruit who puts on his uniform and foolishly imagines that one week of service will ensure a crown of glory. It is a lifelong war—a fight needing the power of every muscle and a strong heart to be triumphant. If we do come off as more than conquerors (Rom. 8:37), it shall be said of us as one has said of Jesus Christ: "He had strength enough and none to spare." It is a battle at which the stoutest heart might quail if he did not remember that the Lord is on his side, and therefore, whom shall he fear? He is the strength of his life; of whom shall he be afraid? This fight with the world is not one of physical might. If it were, we might soon win it. But it is all the more dangerous from the fact that it is a strife of mind, a contest of heart, a struggle of the spirit and soul. When we overcome the world in one fashion, we have not done half of our work, for the world changes it shape continually and is like a chameleon that has all the colors of the rainbow.

When you have beaten the world in one shape, it will attack you in another. Until you die, you will always have new appearances of the world to wrestle. Let me mention some of the forms in which the Christian overcomes the world.

The World as a Legislator

The Christian overcomes the world when the world sets itself up as a legislator, wishing to teach him customs. The world has its old massive law book of accepted customs and fashions and bans anyone who refuses to be conformed to its standard. Most people just do what everyone else does. If they see so-and-so do a dishonest thing in business, it is enough for them that everyone must be doing it. Because the majority of mankind has certain habits, they yield as well. It seems to be based on the thought that to march to hell in crowds will help to diminish the fierce heat of the burning of the bottomless pit, instead of remembering that the more fuel the fiercer the flame. Like dead fish, people usually swim with the stream. It is only the Christian who despises the world's customs and asks, "Is it right or is it wrong? If it is right, I will be true to do it. If there is not another person in this world who will do it, I will do it. Should a 'universal hiss' go up to heaven, I still will do it. Should the very stones of earth fly up and stone me to death, yet will I do it. Though they bind me to a stake, yet must I do it. If the multitude will not follow me, I will go without them. I will be delighted if everyone else does right as well, but if not, I will despise their customs. I shall not be measured by what others do; it is to my own Master I stand or fall." Thus the Christian conquers and overcomes the world.

Fair world! She dresses herself in the robes of a judge and solemnly proclaims, "You are wrong. Look around and see what others do. Behold my laws that have been followed for hundreds of years. Who are you to set yourself up against me?" She pulls out her worm-eaten law book and, turning over the musty pages, says, "See, here is an act passed in the reign of Nebuchadnezzar, and here's one from the days of Pharaoh. These must be right because antiquity has enrolled them among her authorities. Do you mean to set yourself up against the opinions of the multitudes?"

Yes, we do. We take the world's law book and burn it, as the

Ephesians did their magic rolls, turning her decrees into waste-paper. We tear her proclamations from the walls and trample her customs as cobwebs. When being true to God is to be right, we count it the proudest wisdom to be singular. We walk as a distinct people, a separate race, a chosen generation, a peculiar people (1 Pet. 2:9). A Christian cannot live by a double standard but lives to say, "If I pray, I will also act. If I go to the house of God and profess to love God, I love Him everywhere. I take my religion into the shop, behind the counter, and into the office." If it does not travel with us, God knows it is not religion at all. We must stand up, then, against the customs of the world.

The World's Standards

The Christian rebels against the world's customs. And when he does so, the world says, "That man is a heretic, a fool, a fanatic, or a hypocrite." The world grasps her sword and scowls like a demon, then gathers her strength and cries, "The believer dares defy my government. He will not follow those around him. Then I will per-secute him. Slander, come from the depths of hell and hiss at him! Envy, sharpen your tooth and bite him!" She afflicts him wherever he is and however she can. She tries to ruin him in business. If he stands as a champion for the truth, she leaves no stone unturned whereby she may injure him.

What is the behavior of the Lord's warrior when he sees the world take up arms against him and sees all earth, like an army, coming to utterly destroy him? Does he yield or bend or cringe? Oh, no! Like Luther, he writes on his banner, "I yield to none." He goes to war against the world if the world goes to war against him. The true-born child of God cares little for man's opinion. He says, "If need be, let me be doomed to wander the world penniless and even to die. Each drop of blood within these veins belongs to Christ, and I am ready to shed it for His name's sake." He counts all things but loss, that he may win Christ and be found in Him (Phil. 3:8–9). When the world's thunder roars, he smiles and says, "As the lightning that leaps from its thunder lair and splits the clouds and frightens the stars but is powerless against the rock-covered mountaineer, so now the world cannot hurt me. In the time of trouble, my Father hides me in His pavilion, in the secret of His tabernacle He hides me and sets me up upon a rock." Thus, again, we conquer the world by not caring about its frown.

The World's Smile

"Well," the world says, "I will try another approach." And this is the most dangerous of all. A smiling world is worse than a frowning one. She says, "I cannot bring this person down with repeated blows, so I will take off the metal glove and show a fair white hand. I'll bid him kiss it. I will tell him I love him, speaking good words that flatter his soul." John Bunyan describes this in his character Madam Bubble. She has a winning way about her, dropping a smile at the end of each sentence and always talking of fair things. Believe me, Christians are not so much in danger when they are persecuted as when they are admired. When we stand upon the pinnacle of popularity, we may well tremble and fear. It is not when we are ridiculed that we have a cause for alarm but when people speak well of us that we need beware. It is not in the cold wintry wind that I take off my coat of righteousness and throw it away. It is when the sun comes, the weather is warm, and the air is balmy that I let down my guard, take off my robes, and expose myself to the world. How many people have been made naked by the love of this world? The world has flattered and applauded, and the man drinks in the intoxicating draught. He staggers and reels, then he sins and loses his reputation. As a comet that flashes through the sky, wanders far into space, and is lost in darkness, so is the man. Great as he was, he falls. Mighty as he was, he wanders and is lost.

But the true child of God is safe when the world smiles upon him. He cares as little for her praise as for her anger. If he is praised, and it is true, he says, "My deeds deserve praise, but I refer all honor to my God." Great souls know what they merit from their critic; to them it is nothing more than the giving of their daily income. Some people cannot live without a large amount of praise; and if they have no more than they deserve, let them have it. If they are children of God, they will be kept steady. They will not be ruined or spoiled, but they will stand with feet like hinds' feet upon high places. "This is the victory that overcometh the world."

The World as a Jailor

Sometimes the world turns jailor to a Christian. Affliction and sorrow come into a person's life until life becomes a prison, and the world its wretched jailor. Trials and troubles come, and the world makes her approach saying, "Poor prisoner, I have a key that will let you out. You could be free if you but put your conscience away. Never mind him when he says that this would be a dishonest act. Let him sleep. Think about the honesty after you get the money. You can repent later." But you say, "I cannot do the thing." "Well," says the world, "then groan and grumble. A good man like you deserves to be locked up in this prison!" The Christian responds, "My Father has allowed this trouble into my life, and in His own time He will fetch me out. But if I die here, I will not use a wrong means to escape. My Father has put me here for my good, and I will not grumble." "Then you are a fool," says the world. The scorner laughs and passes on, saying, "The man has no brain or courage to launch upon the sea. He wants to go in the old beaten track of morality." Yes, he does, and so he overcomes the world.

Think of the battles that have been fought. There are many who have worked, worked, worked, until their fingers were worn to the bone, to earn a meager living. The temptation has come a thousand times to compromise their integrity, but in the midst of poverty they still stand upright. The promise of riches in an hour, affluence in a moment, if they will but clutch something that God has said no to, has brought its enticement. The world says, "Be rich, be rich," but the Holy Spirit says, "No! Be honest. Serve your God." This is the valiant battle for the heart. The Christian says, "No. Could I have the stars transformed into worlds of gold, I will not compromise my principles and damage my soul." And thus he walks away the conqueror.

A Great Birth

The text speaks of a great birth—something wonderful from God sent into the hearts of men. "For whatsoever is born of God overcometh the world." This new birth is the mysterious point in all religion. If you preach anything else except the new birth, you will always fair well with those who listen. But if you insist that to enter heaven there must be a radical change, though it is the doctrine of Scripture, it is so unpalatable to mankind in general that you will hardly get them to listen. How many have turned away at the sound of "Except a man be born again, he cannot see the kingdom of God" (John 3:3)? If I say there must be a regenerating influence exerted upon a person's mind by the power of the Holy Spirit, there are some who say, "It is just emotionalism." Call it what you may, the Bible declares it. There I stand; by this I will be judged. If the Bible does not say we must be born again, then I give it up. But if it does, do not distrust the truth on which your salvation hangs.

What is it to be born again? Some say it takes place in an infant baptism. Just the mention of it is so absurd that I can scarcely imagine the preachers of it have any brains in their heads. The person who believes it puts himself below the range of a common-sense man. Believe that every child is born again by a drop of water! Believe that thousands of people who sin continuously have been regenerated because those sanctified drops once fell upon their infant forehead! Ridiculous!

To be born again is to undergo a change so *mysterious* that human words cannot speak of it. As we cannot describe our first birth, so it is impossible for us to describe the second. "The wind bloweth where it listeth, and thou hearest the sound thereof, but canst not tell whence it cometh, and whither it goeth: so is every one that is born of the Spirit" (John 3:8). But while it is so mysterious, it is a change that is *known and felt*. It is experienced and felt in a real way. As electricity is mysterious and yet produces a real sensation, so is the new birth. At the time of the new birth, the soul is often in great agony—perhaps drowned in seas of tears. Sometimes it drinks bitters, now and then mingled with sweet drops of hope. While we are passing from death to life, there is an experience that no one but the child of God can understand. It is a mysterious change, but a positive one. It is as much a change as if this heart were taken out of me and the black drops of blood wrung from it, then washed and cleansed and put into my soul again. It is "a new heart . . . and a new spirit" (Ezek. 36:26). That is mysterious, yet an actual and real change!

Moreover, this change is a *supernatural one*. It is not one that a man performs upon himself. It is not by stopping drinking or by going to church or by turning from Catholic to Protestant. It is a new principle infused that works in the heart, enters the very soul, and moves the entire person. It is a renewal of my nature, so that I am not the man I used to be but a new man in Christ Jesus. It is a work of the Spirit of God so mighty and wondrous that no minister's eloquence can bring about. It remains to be confessed to be the work of God, and God alone. Thus it can be said that the new birth is an *enduring change*. The Bible is clear that wherever God begins a good work, He will carry it on even to the end (Phil. 1:6), and that those whom God loves, He loves to the end. If I am really born again through a real supernatural change, I may fall into sin, but I shall not fall finally. I shall stand while life shall last, constantly secure; and when I die, it shall be said, "The battle's fought, the victory's won. Enter your rest of joy."

A Great Grace

Persons who are born again really do overcome the world. How is this brought about? The text says, "This is the victory that overcometh the world, even our *faith*." Christians do not triumph over the world by reason. Reason is a very good thing, and no one should find fault with it. Reason is a candle, but faith is the sun. While I prefer the sun, I do not put out the candle. I use my reason constantly, but when I come to real warfare, reason is a wooden sword. It breaks, it snaps, while faith, that sword of true Jerusalem metal, cuts to the dividing of soul and body. Those who do something significant in the world are always men of faith. The person who wins the battle is the one who knows he will win and vows to be the victor. Those who never get on in this world are those who are always afraid to do a thing for fear they cannot accomplish it. Who climbs to the top of the Alps? The person who says, "I will do it, or I will die." Let such a person make up his mind that he can do a thing, and he will do it if it is within the range of possibility. Those who have lifted the standard and, grasping it with a firm hand, have held it up in the midst of stormy strife and battle are the men of faith. Men of fear and trembling run, but men of faith, whose boldness is etched on their foreheads like brass, lift their eyes "unto the hills, from whence cometh my help" (Ps. 121:1), believing in God.

It has been said that "Never was a marvel done upon the earth, but it had sprung of faith; nothing noble, generous, or great, but faith was the root of the achievement; nothing comely, nothing famous, but its praise is faith." Faith is mightiest of the mighty. It is the monarch of the realms of the mind. There is no being superior to its strength, no creature that will not bow to its divine prowess. The lack of faith makes a person despicable; it shrivels him up so small that he might live in a nutshell. Give him faith, and he is a leviathan that can dive into the depths of the sea, a giant who takes nations and crumbles them in his hand, vanquishing hosts with his sword and gathering up all the crowns as his own. There is nothing like faith. Faith makes you almost as omnipotent as God, by the borrowed power of its divinity. Give us faith and we can do all things.

How is it that faith overcomes the world? The principle is this: "Like cures like." Faith tramples the *fear* of the world by the fear of God. The world says, "If you do not do this and bow before my false god, you shall be put in the fiery furnace." "But," says the man of faith, "I fear him who can destroy both body and soul in hell. True, I may dread you, but I have a greater fear than that. I tremble that I might offend my sovereign Lord." So the one fear counterbalances the other. How does faith overthrow the world's *hopes*? "Take a look at this," says the world. "I will give you all of this if you will be my disciple. There is hope for you. You can be rich and great." But faith says, "I have a hope laid up in heaven; a hope that never fades, eternal, incorrupt, a golden hope, a crown of life." So the hope of glory overcomes all the hopes of the world. "Ah!" says the world. "Why not follow the *example* of those around you?" "Because I follow the example of Christ," faith responds. Faith overcomes example by example. "Well, since you will not be conquered by all this, come, I will *love* you," says the world. "You shall be my friend." Faith says, "He that is the friend of the world cannot be a friend of God. God loves me. What else could I need?" So faith puts love against love, fear against fear, hope against hope, dread against dread, and overcomes the world by "like curing like."

And now, what do you say? Has your faith overcome the

world? Can you live above it? Or do you love the world and its things? Is Jesus worthy of your love? Are the things of eternity and heaven worth the things of time? Is it so sweet to be a worldling that you can risk your soul's eternal welfare? It is vital godliness you need. It is not a religious Sunday you need, but a religious Monday. It is not a pious church, but a holy place of private prayer. It is not a sacred place to kneel, but a holy place to stand in all day long. There must be a change of heart—real, radical, vital, and entire.

I cannot bring you. My words are powerless, my thoughts are weak. Old Adam is too strong for me to draw or drag you from the world. But God speak to your heart. God send the truth home, and then we shall rejoice in your breaking free and overcoming the world!

*A*nother evil principle is our natural tendency to build up our own works. For a time, that pernicious habit is cured by conviction of sin. The sharp axe of the law cuts down the lofty cedar of fleshly confidence and withers all its branches; but since the root still remains, at the very scent of water it sprouts again, and the axe must be set to work again. When we think legalism is quite dead, it revives, and linking hands with our love of change, it tempts us to forsake our simple standing upon Christ, the Rock of Ages. Legalism urges us to advance to something that it decorates before our eyes with fancy colors and appears to our feeble understandings to be better or more honorable to ourselves. Though this will be beaten down by the Christian, for he will meet trouble after trouble when he follows this path, yet again the old secret desire to be something or do something or have some little honor by performing the works of the law will come in, and we shall need to hear the voice of wisdom in our hearts saying, "As ye have therefore received Christ Jesus the Lord, so walk ye in him." We must persevere in the same way that we began. As at the first Christ Jesus was the source of your life, the principle of your actions, and the joy of your spirit, so let Him be the same even until life's end—the same when you walk through the valley of the shadow of death and enter into the joy and the rest that remains for the people of God.

Chapter Eleven

The Life and Walk of Faith

As ye have therefore received Christ Jesus the Lord, so walk ye in him—Colossians 2:6.

HUMAN NATURE IS FOND OF CHANGE. Although man was made in the image of God in the beginning, it is obvious that any trace of immutability that man might once have possessed has long ago departed. If an unrenewed man could possess the joys of heaven, he would in time grow weary of them and crave for change. When the children of Israel in the wilderness were fed on angels' food, they murmured for variety and groaned out, "Our soul loatheth this light bread" (Num. 21:5). It is little wonder, then, that we need cautions against shifting the ground of our hope and the object of our faith.

Another evil principle will co-work with this love of change in our hearts and produce incredible mischief—our natural tendency to build up our own works. For a time, that pernicious habit is cured by conviction of sin. The sharp axe of the law cuts down the lofty cedar of fleshly confidence and withers all its branches; but since the root still remains, at the very scent of water it sprouts again, and the axe must be set to work again. When we think legalism is quite dead, it revives, and linking hands with our love of change, it tempts us to forsake our simple standing upon Christ, the Rock of Ages. Legalism urges us to advance to something that it decorates before our eyes with fancy colors and appears to our feeble understandings to be better or more honorable to ourselves. Though this will be beaten down by the Christian, for he will meet trouble after trouble when he follows this path, yet again the old secret desire to be something or do something or have some little honor by performing the works of the law will come in, and we shall need to hear the voice of wisdom in our hearts saying, "As ye have therefore received Christ Jesus the Lord, so walk ye in him." We must persevere in the same way that we began. As at the first Christ Jesus was the source of your life, the principle of your actions, and the joy of your spirit, so let Him be the same even until life's end—the same when you walk through the valley of the shadow of death and enter into the joy and the rest that remains for the people of God.

An Exposition of Colossians 2:6

In the plainest possible language, and by the gracious Spirit who alone can lead us into all truth, I would endeavor to open up this verse. The text is easily broken into two parts: here is, first, the life of faith—receiving Christ Jesus the Lord; here is, second, the walk of faith—so walk ye in Him.

The Life of Faith

The Holy Spirit first reveals to us *the life of faith*—the way by which we are saved. Note carefully that it is represented as *receiving*. The word *implies the very opposite of anything like merit*. Merit is purchasing, making by labor, or winning by valor. Receiving is just the accepting of a thing as a gift. The eternal life that God gives His people is in no sense the fruit of our working; it is the gift of God. As the earth drinks in the rain, as the sea receives the streams, as night accepts light from the stars, so we, giving nothing, partake freely of the grace of God. The saints are not by nature wells or streams; they are but cisterns into which the living water flows. As empty vessels, sovereign mercy puts them under the pipe, and they receive grace upon grace until they are filled to the brim. It is a fatal mistake to talk about winning salvation by works, prayers, tears, penance, mortification of the flesh, or zealous obedience to the law. The very first principle of the divine life is not giving out but receiving. What comes from Christ into me is that which is my salvation, not that which springs out of my own heart. My nature must be renewed and changed by that which comes from the divine Redeemer.

The idea of receiving implies *a sense of realization*, making the matter *a reality*. One cannot receive a shadow; we receive that which is substantial. Gold, silver, and precious stones are things we can receive. Bread, water, food, clothing, and riches are substances that are possible for us to receive. We do not receive a dream or a shadow or a phantom. There is something real in a thing that is received. The same is true in the life of faith—we realize Christ. Before faith comes, Christ is a name to us, a person who may have lived long ago, so long ago that His life is only a history to us now. By an act of faith, Christ becomes a real person in the consciousness of our heart, as real to us as our own flesh and blood. We speak of Christ and think of Him as we would our brother, our father, our friend. Our faith gives substance to the history and idea of Christ, putting real solidity into the spirit and name of Christ. Our life in Christ becomes to us a thing to taste and handle, to lay hold upon and to receive as real and true. This becomes the one grand reality— that God is in Christ reconciling you to Himself.

Receiving means also a third thing, that is *getting a grip of it, grasping it*. The thing that I receive becomes my own. I may believe it is real, but that is not receiving it. I may believe, also, that if I ever do get it, it must be given to me, and that I cannot earn it for myself, but that still is not receiving it. Receiving is the bona fide taking into my hand and appropriating to myself as my own property that which is given to me. This is precisely what the soul does when it believes in Christ. Christ becomes *my* Christ: His blood cleanses my sin, and I am cleansed; His righteousness covers me, and I am clothed with it; His Spirit fills me, and I am made to live by it. He becomes to me as much mine as anything that I can call my own. Indeed, what I call my own here on earth is not mine but is only lent to me and will be taken from me. But Christ is so mine that neither life, nor death, nor things present, nor things to come, shall ever be able to rob me of Him (Rom. 8:38). I trust that you, dear reader, can look into the face of Christ and say, "*My* beloved, who loved *me* and gave Himself for *me*. The blessings and promises of the Lord my God are all my own. Whatever I read of in the covenant of grace I hear a voice say in my ears, 'Lift up now thine eyes, and look to the north, and the south, to the east, and to the west—all this have I given *thee* to be thy possession for ever and ever by a covenant of salt.' "

The word *receive* is used in nearly a dozen senses in holy Scripture. To receive is often used for *taking*. We read of receiving a thousand shekels of silver and of receiving money, garments, sheep, and oxen. Perhaps in this sense we understand the words, "A man can receive nothing, except it be given him from heaven" (John 3:27), and that other sentence, "But as many as received him, to them gave he power to become the sons of God" (John 1:12). As the empty vessel takes in water from the stream, so we receive Christ. The love, life, merit, nature, and grace of Jesus freely flow into us.

But the word is also used in Scripture to signify *holding that which we take in*. Indeed, a vessel without a bottom could hardly be said to receive water. The life of faith consists in holding within us that which Christ has put into us, so that Jesus Christ is formed in us the hope of glory. By faith it comes in and by faith it is kept in; faith makes it mine and keeps it mine; faith gets hold of it with one hand and then clasps it with both hands with a grasp that nothing can loose.

Sometimes receiving means in Scripture simply *believing*. "He came unto his own, and his own received him not" (John 1:11). We read of receiving false prophets, that is, believing them. To receive Christ is to believe Him. He says, "I can save you"—I receive that. He says, "Trust me and I will make you like I am"—I receive that. Whatever Jesus says, I believe Him and receive Him as true. I make His word so true to myself that I act upon it as being true, even if heaven and earth should pass away. This is receiving Christ—believing what He has said.

Receiving, also, often signifies in Scripture *entertaining*. Thus, the uncivilized people of Melita received Paul and his companions kindly and kindled a fire (Acts 28:2). After we have found all in Christ to be our own and have received Him into ourselves by faith, we entreat the Lord to enter our hearts and live with us. We give

Him the best seat at the table of our souls. We would feast Him on the richest dainties of our choicest love. We ask Him to abide with us from morning to night. We would commune with Him every day and hour. Receiving Christ is to entertain Him.

Receiving in Scripture often signifies *to enjoy*. We hear of receiving a crown of life that never fades away—that is, enjoying it, enjoying heaven, and being satisfied with all its bliss. When we receive Christ, there is intended in this an enjoying of it. I am only talking here of the simplicities of the faith, but I do want to make them personal to you. Are you enjoying Christ? If you had a crown, you would wear it. If you were hungry and there was food on the table, you would eat it. Oh, eat and drink of your Lord Jesus Christ! If you have a friend, you enjoy his company. You have a friend in Christ—enjoy His friendship! Do not leave Him like a sealed-up bottle or some choice dainty all untasted. Receive Christ, for this is the very heaven and rest of the soul. Come and delight yourselves in Him. To take Him into one's self, to hold Him there, to believe every word He says, to entertain Him in one's heart, and to enjoy the luscious sweetness that He confers upon all who have eaten His flesh and have been made to drink His blood—this is to receive Christ.

But we have not yet brought out the real meaning of this life of faith until we dwell upon another word. "As ye have received." Received what? Salvation may be described as the blind receiving sight, the deaf receiving hearing, the dead receiving life. But there is more to get hold of. "As ye have received *Christ Jesus the Lord*." Do you catch it? It is true that He gave us life from the dead, pardon from sin, and imputed righteousness. These are priceless things, but you see we are not content with them—we have received *Christ Himself*. The Son of God has been poured out into us, and we have received Him. Not merely the blessings of the covenant, but *Himself*; not merely the purchase of His blood, but He Himself from whose veins the blood has flowed has become ours. Every soul that has eternal life is this day a possessor of Christ Jesus the Lord.

Have I received *Christ* the *anointed*? My soul, have you seen Christ as the anointed of the Father in the divine decree to execute His purposes? Have you seen Him coming forth in the fullness of time wearing the robes of His priesthood? Have you seen Him standing at the altar offering Himself as a victim, an anointed priest, anointed with the sacred oil by which God has made him a priest forever after the order of Melchisedec? My soul, have you seen Jesus go within the veil and speak to my Father and to His Father as one whom the Father has accepted, of whom we can speak, in the language of David, as our shield and God's anointed? It is a delight indeed to receive Christ not as an unsent prophet who came of his own authority, not as a teacher who spoke his own word, but as one who is *Christos*, the anointed of God, ordained of the Most High, and therefore most certainly acceptable. As it is written, "He hath borne our griefs, and carried our sorrows: yet we did esteem him stricken, smitten of God, and afflicted. But he was wounded for our transgressions, he was bruised for our iniquities: the chastisement of our peace was upon him; and with his stripes we are healed" (Isa. 53:4–5). Delightful is the contemplation of Christ! Soul, have you received the Messiah of God?

But the text says, "Christ *Jesus*." Jesus means a Savior. *Christ* is His relation to God, *Jesus* His relation to me. There are some who profess salvation who do not seem to have received Christ as *Jesus*. They look upon Him as One who may help them to save themselves, who can do a great deal for them, or may begin the work but not complete it. We must get ahold of Him as one who has saved us, who has finished the work. Do we doubt today that we are whiter than the driven snow because His blood has washed us? We are more acceptable to God than unfallen angels ever were, for we are clothed in the perfect righteousness of a divine one. Christ has wrapped you about with His righteousness. See that you receive Him as Jesus your Savior.

It is also clear that saving faith consists in receiving Him *as He is in Himself, as the divine Son.* "Ye have received Christ Jesus *the Lord.*" Those who say they cannot believe in His deity have not received Him. Nor is it to theoretically admit Him to be divine. The soul must say, "I take Him into my heart as being God over all, blessed forever, Amen. I kiss His feet while I see His humanity. But I believe that since those feet could tread the waters, He is divine. I look up to His hands, and as I see them pierced, I know that He is human. But as I know that those hands multiplied the loaves and fishes until they fed five thousand, I know that He is divine. I look upon His corpse in the tomb, and I see that He is man. I see Him in the resurrection, and I know that He is God. I see Him suffering on the cross, and I know that He is bone of my bone and flesh of my flesh. But I hear a voice that says, 'Let all the angels of God worship Him' (Heb. 1:6); 'Thy throne, O God, is for ever and ever' (Heb. 1:7); and I bow before Him and say, 'O Lord, Son of God and Son of Mary, I receive You as Christ Jesus *the Lord.'* "

The apostle speaks of this *as a matter of certainty,* and he goes on to argue from it. We do not argue from supposition. Unless you can say, "I have received Jesus," the rest will make no sense—"so walk ye in him." We must not alter it into, "Since *I hope* I have." If you have not received Him, humble yourself under the mighty hand of God and cry to Him for His great gift.

The Walk of Faith

The second point of the text was *the walk of faith.* "Since ye have received him, walk in him." Walk implies, first of all, *action.* Do not let your reception of Christ be a mere thing of thought to you, but act upon it all. If you have received Christ, act as if you were saved—with joy, meekness, confidence, faith, and boldness. Walk in Him; do not sit down in indolence but rise and act in Him. Carry out into practical effect that which you believe. Act as the man who has received an immense fortune and behaves like a rich man. Do not play the beggar now that boundless wealth is conferred upon you.

Walking also implies *perseverance,* not only being in Christ today but also being in Him tomorrow, and the next day, and the next, and the next. It means walking in Him all your walk of life. I remember Matthew Henry, speaking about Enoch walking with God, say he did not take only a turn or two up and down with God and then leave Him, but Enoch walked with God four hundred years. That is perseverance. Persevere in receiving Christ. You have come to trust Him—keep trusting Him.

Walking implies *habit.* When we speak of a man's walk and conversation, we mean his habits, the constant tenor of his life. It is not to occasionally enjoy Christ and then to forget Him. Let it be your habit to live upon Him; keep to Him; cling to Him; never let Him go, but live and have your being in Him.

This walking implies *a continuance.* There must be a continual abiding in Christ. How many Christians there are who think that in the morning and evening they should come into the company of Christ, and then they may be in the world all day long. We should always be in Christ—all the day long, every minute of the day. Though worldly things may take up some of my thoughts, yet my soul is to be in a constant state of being in Christ. At any moment my life will give evidence to the fact that I am joined to Christ. We proceed from grace to grace, running forward until we reach the uttermost limit of knowledge that man can have concerning our Beloved.

Please notice that it says, "Walk ye *in him.*" I cannot attempt to enter into the mystery contained. Just as we walk in the air, so we are to walk in Christ as our element. Can you comprehend that? Without the dynamic of inner spiritual life, there will be no understanding of what it means to have fellowship with the Father and His Son Jesus Christ. In trying to open up that point just for a moment, let us notice what this walking in Christ must mean. As Christ was *the only ground of our faith* when we received Him, so as long as we live, we are to stand to the same point. We commence our faith with "Nothing in my hand I bring, Simply to the cross I cling," and we finish our walk and service of faith singing the same tune.

Let not your experience, your sanctification, your graces, your attainments, come between you and Christ. Just as you took Him to be the only pillar of your hope at first, so let Him be even to the last. You received Christ as *the substance of your faith.* Unbelievers laughed at you and said you had nothing to trust, but your faith made Christ real to you. Just as the first day when you came to Jesus you no more doubted the reality of Christ, so walk in Him. I can well recollect that first moment when my eyes looked to Christ! There was never anything so true to me as those bleeding hands or that thorn-crowned head. I wish it were always so, and indeed it should be. And that day Christ became to us *the joy of our souls.* Home, friends, health, wealth, comforts—all lost their luster that day when He appeared, just as stars are hidden by the light of the sun. He was the only Lord and giver of life's best bliss, the only well of living water springing up unto everlasting life. I know that the first day it did not matter to me whether the day itself was gloomy or bright. I had found Christ—that was enough for me. He was my Savior, my all. Just as you received Him at first as your only joy, so receive Him still, walking in Him, making Him the source, the center, and the circumference to all of your soul's range of delight.

So, that day when we received Him, we received Him as *the object of our love*. How we loved Christ then! Had we met Him that day, we would have broken the alabaster box of precious ointment and poured it upon His head. We would have washed His feet with our tears and wiped them with the hairs of our head. Ah, Jesus, when I first received you, I thought I should have behaved far better than I have. I thought I would spend and be spent for You, that I would never dishonor You nor turn aside from my faith and devotedness. But, alas, I have not come up to the standard of our text—walking with Him as I have received Him. He has not been by us so well beloved as we dreamed He would have been.

Advocating the Principle of Faith

If we have been saved by Christ but then begin to walk in someone or something else, what then? *We bring dishonor to our Lord.* Here is a man who came to Christ, but after relying upon the Lord some half a dozen years, he begins to walk by feelings, sight, philosophy, or carnal wisdom. What discredit does it bring upon our Holy Leader and Captain? I am certain, though, that if you have tasted that the Lord is gracious, that He is a compassionate and generous friend, that simple faith in Him has given you all the peace your spirit could desire, you will not stain His glory in the dust and walk away from Him.

Besides, *what reason do you have to make a change*? Has Christ not proven Himself all-sufficient? When you have dared to come as a guilty sinner and believed in Him, have you ever been ashamed? Very well, then, let the past urge you to walk in Him. And as for *the present*, can that compel you to leave Christ? When we are hard beset with this world or with the severer trials within the Church, we find it such a sweet thing to come back and pillow our head upon the bosom of our Savior. This is the joy we have today, that we are in Him, and if we find this today to be enough, why would we think of changing? No brighter Lover of my soul can ever appear. I will hold Him with an immortal grasp and bind His name as a seal upon my arm. As for the *future,* can you suggest anything that can arise that shall render it necessary for you to strike sail or go with another captain in another ship? I think not. To those near death, is it not written that "neither death, nor life, nor angels, nor principalities, nor powers, nor things present, nor things to come, shall be able to separate us from the love of God, which is in Christ Jesus our Lord" (Rom. 8:38–39). To those who are poor, what better than to have a Christ who can make them rich in faith? Suppose you are mistreated, mocked, and slandered for Jesus' sake—what better do you want than to have Him as a friend who sticketh closer than a brother? In life, in death, in judgment, you cannot conceive anything that can arise in which you would require more than Christ bestows.

It may be that you are tempted by something else to change your course for a time. What is it? Is it the wisdom of this world, the cunning devices and discoveries of man? Is it that which our apostle mentions as philosophy? The wise men of the world have persuaded you to begin questioning, urging you to put the mysteries of God to the test of common sense, reason, and so forth, as they call it, and not lean on the inspiration of God's Word. It may be wisdom that they suppose philosophy offers you, but have you not that in Christ, "in whom are hid all the treasures of wisdom and knowledge" (Col. 2:3)? You received Christ at first as being made of God unto you wisdom, and sanctification, and righteousness, and so on (1 Cor. 1:30). Will you cast Him off when you have already more than all the wisdom that philosophy could possibly offer?

Is it *ceremonies* that tempt you? Have you been told that you must attend certain meetings, and then you would have another ground of confidence? I am here to say that you have that in Christ. If there is anything in the circumcision of the Jews, you have that, for you are circumcised in Christ (Col. 2:11). If there is anything in baptism, you have been buried with Him in baptism (Col. 2:12). Do you want life? Your life is hid with Him (Col. 3:3). Do you want death? You are dead with Christ and buried with Him (Col. 2:12). Do you want resurrection? He has raised you up with Him (Col. 3:1). Do you want heaven? He has made you sit together in heavenly places in Him (Eph. 2:6). Getting Christ, you have all that everything else can offer you. Therefore, do not be tempted from this hope of your calling. But as you have received Christ, so walk in Him.

Further, do you not know this? Your Jesus is the Lord from heaven. *What can your heart desire* beyond God? God is infinite; you cannot want more than the infinite. "In him dwelleth all the fulness of Godhead bodily" (Col. 2:9). Having Christ, you have God, and having God, you have everything. Well might the apostle add to that sentence, "And ye are complete in him." If you are complete in Christ, why should you be fooled by the bewitcheries of this world to want something besides Christ? If resting upon Him, God is absolutely yours, and you are, therefore, full to the brim with all that your largest capacity can desire, how could you be led astray like a foolish child to see another's confidence and trust? Come back, you who wander. Come back to the solid foundation of which we sing: "On Christ the solid rock I stand, All other ground is sinking sand."

Faith Applied

"So walk ye in him." One of the first applications shall be made with regard to those who complain of a lack of communion with Christ. The application of the principle of faith is that as you have received Him, so walk in Him. If it was worthwhile for you to come to Him at first, it is worthwhile for you always to keep to Him. If it was the foundation of blessedness to you to simply come to Christ, it will be a fountain of blessedness to you to do the same now. Come, then, to Him *now*. Do not be so foolish as to not stand by Christ now. Come, let the remembrance of your marriage to the Lord Jesus restore you. If you have lost your fellowship with Jesus, come again to His dear body wounded, for your sake, and say, "Lord Jesus, help me from this time forth as I have received You, day by day to walk in You."

Many complain for *a lack of comfort*. Sin has broken in and disturbed your faith. But how did you receive Christ? As a saint? "No, no," say you, "I came to Christ as a sinner." So, come to Him as a sinner now. "Oh, but I feel so guilty!" Just so, but what was your hope at first? Why, guilty though you were, He had made an atonement, and you trusted in Him. Do the same as you did at first.

Walking in Him, I cannot imagine a person without comfort who continually makes this the strain of his life, to rest on Christ as a poor sinner. Lord, You know the devil often says to me, "You are no saint." Well, then, if I am not a saint, yet I am a sinner, and it is written "Jesus Christ came into the world to save sinners" (1 Tim. 1:15). You cannot help having comfort if you walk with your Savior as you did at the first, resting in Him, and not in feelings, nor experience, nor graces, nor anything of your own. Living and resting alone in Him who is made of God unto you all that your soul requires is comfort indeed.

There is yet another thing. There are many Christians whose lives really *are not consistent.* I cannot understand this if they are walking with Christ. We hear of one who exaggerates to the point of telling lies and of another who is constantly impatient, always troubled, fretting, mournful. If the person is really walking in Christ, how can he be doubting the goodness, the providence, the tenderness of God. Surely he is not. I have heard of hard-hearted, stingy believers who refuse to help their needy brethren. Are they walking in Christ when they do that? To walk in Christ leads to actions like Christ. Being in Christ, a person's hope, love, joy, and life are the reflection of the image of Christ. He is the glass into which Christ looks. Others look at that man and say, "He is like his Master. He lives in Christ."

If we lived now as we did the first day we came to Christ, we should live very differently from what we do. How does He feel toward His Father? How does He feel toward sinners? Do we feel something of the same? On that first day when we were on our knees, what pleading there was with Him, what a nearness of access to Him in prayer! How different today. This world has with a rude hand brushed the bloom from the young fruit. Is it true that flowers of grace, like the flowers of nature, die in the autumn of our godliness? As we get older, should we become more worldly? Should our early love die away? Forgive, O Lord, this evil, and turn us afresh to You.

Christ is free and full, full to give you all that you need and free to give it even to you. Trust in God's anointed—that is, receive Him—and then, having trusted Him, continue still to trust Him. May His Spirit enable you to do it, and to His name shall be glory forever and ever.

Do not think that as you grow in grace the path will become smoother beneath your feet and the heavens serener above your head. Reckon that as God gives you greater skill as a soldier, He will send you upon more arduous enterprises. As He more fully equips your vessel to brave the tempest and the storm, so He will send you out upon more boisterous seas and upon longer voyages that you may honor Him and still further increase your holy confidence. You would have thought that Abraham had come to the land Beulah, that in his old age, after the birth of Isaac and expulsion of Ishmael, he would have had a time of perfect rest. Let this warn us that we are never to reckon upon rest from tribulation this side of the grave. No, the clarion still sounds the note of war. We may not sit down and celebrate our victory as yet. We must still wear the helmet and bear the sword and watch and pray and fight, expecting that the last battle may be the worst and that the fiercest charge of the foe may be reserved for the end of the day.

Chapter Twelve

Mature Faith

And he said, Take now thy son, thine only son Isaac, whom thou lovest, and get thee into the land of Moriah; and offer him there for a burnt offering upon one of the mountains which I will tell thee of—Genesis 22:2.

THE LESSONS THAT CENTER ON THE FAITH of Abraham are innumerable, but my purpose with this verse is to dwell upon the triumph of Abraham's faith when his spiritual life had come to the highest point of maturity. Abraham had endured the severest of many ordeals, each most searching and remarkable. It was "after these things" (Gen. 22:1)—after he had passed through a great fight of affliction and through it had been strengthened and sanctified—that Abraham was called to endure a still sterner test. God does not put heavy burdens upon weak shoulders. He educates our faith, testing it by trials that increase little by little in proportion as our faith has increased. He expects us to do a man's work and to endure man's affliction only when we have passed through the childhood state and arrived at the stature of men in Christ Jesus. Expect then that your trials will multiply as you proceed toward heaven.

Do not think that as you grow in grace the path will become smoother beneath your feet and the heavens serener above your head. Reckon that as God gives you greater skill as a soldier, He will send you upon more arduous enterprises. As He more fully equips your vessel to brave the tempest and the storm, so He will send you out upon more boisterous seas and upon longer voyages that you may honor Him and still further increase your holy confidence. You would have thought that Abraham had come to the land Beulah, that in his old age, after the birth of Isaac and expulsion of Ishmael, he would have had a time of perfect rest. Let this warn us that we are never to reckon upon rest from tribulation this side of the grave. No, the clarion still sounds the note of war. We may not sit down and celebrate our victory as yet. We must still wear the helmet and bear the sword and watch and pray and fight, expecting that the last battle may be the worst and that the fiercest charge of the foe may be reserved for the end of the day.

Let us study the greatest trial of Abraham's life, remembering that God was pleased to give it as an example for all believers.

The Trial Itself

Every syllable of the text is significant. Every single syllable of God's address to Abraham seems intended to pierce the patriarch to the deepest parts. "Take now *thy son*." What! A father slay his son? Was there nothing in Abraham's tent that God would have but his son? Abraham would cheerfully have given sheep and cattle, all the silver and gold he possessed, but his son? How this tugs at the father's heartstrings! Will God be content with a proof of his obedience only by the surrender of the fruit of his body? The word *only* is made particularly emphatic by the fact that Ishmael had been exiled at the command of God. If Isaac shall die, there is no other descendant left, and no probability of another to succeed him. The light of Abraham will be quenched, and his name forgotten. Sarah and he are very old. No infant's cry will again gladden the tent. Isaac is his only son, a lone star of the night, the lamp of his father's old age.

Nor is that all: "Thine only son, *Isaac*." What a multitude of memories that word *Isaac* stirred in Abraham's mind. This was the child of promise, of a promise full of grace, of a promise the fulfillment of which was anxiously expected, but long, long, long delayed. Isaac, who made his parents' hearts to laugh, the child of the covenant, the boy in whom the father's hopes all centered, for he had been assured, "In Isaac shall thy seed be called" (Gen. 21:12). Must the covenant of God be nullified and the channel of promised blessings be dried up forever?

Yet was it added: *"whom thou lovest."* Must Abraham be reminded of his love at the same time he was told he must lose him? It is a word that seems devoid of compassion. Was it not enough to take away the loved one without awakening Abraham's affections? Isaac was truly beloved of his father, for in addition to the ties of nature and his being the gift of God's grace, Isaac's character was most lovely. Isaac's behavior on the occasion of his sacrifice proves that in his spirit there was an abundance of humility, obedience, resignation, and gentleness. Everything that makes up the beauty of holiness was quite sure to have won the admiration of his father Abraham, whose spiritual eye was well qualified to discern the excellencies that shone in his beloved son. Why must Isaac die? And die, too, by his father's hand? Trial of trials! Contemplative imagination and sympathetic emotion can better depict the father's grief than any words that are in my power to use. I cast a veil where I cannot paint a picture.

Not only was this tender father to lose the best of sons, but he was to lose the son *by his own hand.* It seemed to say, "Abraham, you must be the priest. Your own hand must grasp the sacrificial knife. You must stand there with breaking heart to drive the knife into the breast of your son and see him consumed, even to ashes on the altar." Abraham, the friend of God, was tried in such a way as probably never fell to the lot of man before or since.

In addition to the sacrifice, Abraham was commanded to go to the mountain that God would show him. It is easy on the spur of the moment and under the influence of sacred impulse to perform a heroic deed of self-sacrifice. But it is not so easy for men of passions to deliberate over the sacrifices demanded of us. But Abraham had three days to chew this bitter pill. He must journey on with that dear son before his eyes all the day, listening to that voice so soon to be silent and gazing into those bright eyes so soon to swim with tears and be dimmed by death. Three days of beholding in Isaac his mother's joy and his own delight, yet all the while meditating upon that fatal stroke which, so far as he knew, God required of him. This laying siege to us by long and careful barricade is that which tries us. Only faith, mighty faith, could have assisted him to look in the face the grim trial that now assailed him.

The patriarch was no doubt deeply troubled by the painful suggestions that must have arisen in his heart. "To offer up my child is horrible! Murderous! How can God ask me to do that which runs counter to the whole of my noblest humanity?" Believers are sometimes commanded to come out of the world by deliberate acts that provoke the anger and hatred of those who are nearest and dearest to them. Many a father, mother, husband, wife, brother, or sister has turned away from a believer who is obeying God. Though believers will ever be among the tenderest hearted of men, they count their allegiance to God such that they must give up all for His sake rather than violate the divine law. Perhaps you are suffering under the loss of affection of one dearer to you than life, for whom you could have been well content to die. Learn with Abraham to not let Isaac stand before God. Let Isaac be dear, but let Isaac die sooner than God should be distrusted. This was a main part of Abraham's trial—that it appeared to rudely crush all the tenderest outgrowths of the heart.

It may have suggested itself to Abraham that this would render all the promise of God futile. It is a severe trial for a man to believe and value a promise from God and then do anything that might render it of no effect. Yet there are times when we are called to a course of action that looks as though it will jeopardize our highest hopes. We are sometimes duty bound to perform an action that will, to all appearance, destroy our future usefulness. But it is neither your business nor mine to fulfill God's promise. Though He dash my reputation into shivers and cast my usefulness to the four winds, yet if duty calls me, I must not hesitate a single second in disobedience. At the word of God, Isaac must be offered, though the heavens fall, and faith must answer all the questions by the assurance that what God ordains can never produce anything but good. Obedience can never endanger blessings, for commands are never in real conflict with promises, and God can raise up Isaac and fulfill His own decree.

Further, Abraham must have considered that the death of Isaac was the destruction of all his comfort. The tent shall be darkened for Sarah, and the plain of Mamre shall become as barren as a wilderness of her lamenting heart. Alas for the poor parent who has lost the hope of his old age. The sun grows black at noon, and the moon is eclipsed in darkness if Isaac dies. Better that all calamities should have happened than this dear child be taken away! Abraham must have felt this, but it did not make him hesitate. It may be that doing right will involve a succession of sorrows all but endless, but you must do right, come what may. If the Lord bids you, you must seek the faith to do it, though from that moment, never should another joy make your heart glad until you are fully compensated for the loss by entering into the joy of your Lord at last.

Abraham must have also considered that from that time forth he would make many enemies. Wherever he went he would be shunned as the murderer of his own child. How could he bear to meet Sarah again? "Where is my son?" she would plead. How could he meet his servants again? How could he face Abimelech and the Philistines, who would hear of this strange massacre and shudder at the thought of the monster who defiled the earth on which he trod. Yet the man of faith did not hesitate. What did it matter to him what they thought? Let them count him the devil. Let a universal hiss consign him to the lowest hell of hatred and contempt. God's will must be done. God will take care of his servant's character, or if He does not, His servant must suffer the consequences for the Lord's sake.

This is one of the grandest points about the faith of the father of the faithful. If you and I are called to do the same, may we have the courage to brave reproach with gladness through the power of the Holy Spirit. How Luther's lips must have trembled when he ventured to say that the Pope was Antichrist. Millions bowed to the Pope as the vicar of God on earth. When Luther found himself shunned by the ecclesiastics who once had courted his company and heard the common howl that went up with the vilest insults, he must have felt his ears burn and his cheeks grow red. Yet Luther could feel, "They may call me what they will, but I know that God has spoken unto my soul the great truth that man is to be saved by faith in Jesus Christ and not by ceremonies which the Pope ordains nor the indulgences which he grants; and if my name be consigned to the limbo of the infernal, yet still will I speak out the truth which I know, and in God's name I will not hold my tongue." We must be willing to put aside the verdict of our times and to stand alone, if need be, in the midst of a howling and infuriated world to do honor to the command of God. The only necessity to us is to obey God, even though it bring us shame or death itself.

Abraham's faith was perfected in the severest of outward circumstances and then in the midst of suggestions that were peculiarly perplexing. He put aside both and dared defy both that he might without delay fulfill his Master's will to the full extent. Abraham firmly believed that no evil would come of it, but that he would be more blessed and God more glorified.

The Patriarch Under the Trial

In Abraham's countenance during this test, everything is delightful. Abraham's obedience is a picture of all the virtues in one, blended in marvelous harmony. It would be a shame to mar the effect of the whole sacred deed by mentioning every detail. As details are given, try to keep the whole scene in front of you.

First notice the *submission* of Abraham under this temptation. There is no record kept of any answer that Abraham gave to God. I suppose, therefore, that there was none. One would expect him to have said, "Lord, I know that a human sacrifice cannot be pleasing to you. You cannot take delight in the blood of my dear son. It cannot be." But there is not a word of argument or question or even a prayer of entreaty. He does not ask to escape or to be delivered when he once knows God's will. Abraham goes about the whole business as if he had been ordered only to sacrifice a lamb from the flock. There is a coolness of deliberation that reflects he was gigantic in his faith. "He staggered not," says the apostle (Rom. 4:20), and that is the perfect word. He knows that God commands him, and with awful sternness and yet childlike simplicity, he sets about the task.

The lesson I gather from this is that when you know a duty, never pray to be excused, but go and do it in God's name and in the power of faith. If you clearly see your Master's will, do not begin to argue with it or wait for better opportunities. Do it at once. Some have missed a great deal of joy and honor by the evil habit of temporizing their consciences. It is a terrible thing to begin to let the conscience grow hard, for it soon sears as with a hot iron. Once the conscience is seared and grows hard and unfeeling, it can bear up with a weight of iniquity. Never delay obedience under the pretense of prayer. If professing believers were but jealous for the glory of God and exact and precise in all their walkings before the Most High, they would have more of the honor, more of the blessedness of Abraham, and their influence upon the world would be more like salt and less like the leaven that corrupts the mass.

We must pass on to notice Abraham's *prudence*. Prudence may be a great virtue but often becomes one of the meanest and most beggarly of vices. The prudence of Abraham was seen in his not consulting Sarah about what he was to do. Prudence would have said, "This is a strange command. At least discuss it with Sarah and take her judgment in the case. Moreover, there is that good man Eliezer. He could give you wise counsel." "Yes," Abraham probably thought, "but these loved ones may weaken me." Therefore, like Paul, he did not consult flesh and blood (Gal. 1:16). After all, what is the good of consulting when we know the Lord's mind? If the Bible very plainly states that a certain thing is my duty, for me to consult with man is to question the Majesty of heaven. When God commands, we have nothing left but to obey.

Notice, further, Abraham's *alacrity*. He rose up early in the morning. Delay was not in the patriarch's mind. Is it not grand? The holy man rises early. He will let his God see that he can trust Him and that he will do His bidding without reluctance. He showed his alacrity again by the fact that he prepared the wood himself. It expressly says that he "clave the wood" (Gen. 22:3). Abraham was a mighty man with many servants in his camp, but he became a wood splitter, thinking no work menial if done for God and reckoning the work too sacred for other hands. With a splitting heart he cleaves the wood. Wood for the burning of his heir and dear child! It may be ours to obey God with such a ready zeal of loving children of a Father whom we count it our highest joy to serve, even if that service should involve the sacrifice of our dearest Isaac.

Further, I ask you to notice Abraham's *forethought*. He did everything it would take to consummate the work. Some people take no forethought about serving God, and then if a little hitch occurs, they cry out that it is a providential circumstance and excuse themselves from the unpleasant task. It is amazing the excuses we come up with. One says, "You know, we must make a living." Another asks, "Why should I throw myself out of such an opportune place for such a small matter of conscience?" Abraham thoughtfully takes care as far as possible to forestall all difficulties that might prevent his doing right.

Observe also *Abraham's perseverance.* He continues three days journeying toward the place where he was as much to sacrifice himself as to sacrifice his child. He bids his servants remain where they were, fearful lest they might be moved by pity to prevent the sacrifice. The good man puts everything aside that may prevent his going to the end. Then he puts the wood on Isaac. What a load he must have placed on his own heart as he lay the burden on his dear son! He carried the censer at his side, but what a fire consumed his heart! How intense was the trial when the son innocently said, "Behold the fire and the wood: but where is the lamb for a burnt offering?" (Gen. 22:7). Was there no tear for the patriarch to brush away? We have every reason to believe that Abraham explained to his son what it was that God had commanded, for it is difficult to suppose that Isaac would have blindly yielded without any explanation. Yet through the majesty of the faith he pushes aside his feelings to fulfill the calling of God.

See him now! See the holy man gather up the loose stones that lie upon Mount Moriah! See him take them, and with the help of his son, place them one upon another until the altar has been built. Do you see him lay the wood upon the altar? No signs of flurry or trepidation. See him bind his son with cords! Oh, what cords were those binding his poor heart! *Now* he unsheaths the knife, and the deed is about to be done, but God is content. Abraham has truly sacrificed his son in his heart, and the command is fulfilled. Abraham's faith was practical and heroic. Not only must we love God so as to hope that we should be ready to give up all for Him, but we must be literally and actually ready to do it. We must ask for more faith so that when the trial comes, we shall be proven not to have been mere windbags but to have been true to God in very deed. How many say they love God until it comes to losing something precious. They will obey God until it involves the loss of finances. They will be faithful until it comes to scoffing and shame.

God is no God of theirs except to talk about.

At the bottom of it all, the writer of Hebrews tells us that it was *"by faith* Abraham, when he was tried, offered up Isaac" (11:17). What was the faith that enabled Abraham to do this? I believe that Abraham felt in his own mind that God could not lie and that God's word could not fail, and therefore he could hope to see Isaac raised from the dead. We are told that Abraham believed in God that He could raise Isaac from the dead. Only such a faith could sustain Abraham. Deep down in Abraham's heart was a conviction that by some means God would justify him in what he was to do and that in doing he could not possibly suffer the loss of the promise made in regard to Isaac. In some way, God would take care of him if he did but faithfully keep to God.

Believe that all things work together for good and if by conscience and God's Word you are commanded to do that which would make you poor or cast you into disrepute, it cannot be a real hurt to you. Oh, for the faith that will never fly from the field under any persuasion or compulsion. The faith of Abraham says, "If I die and rot, I will not sin. Come what may, I will not violate my conscience or fail to do what God commands me to perform!"

The Blessings of Obedience

I note at least seven blessings that came to Abraham through the trial of his faith.

First, *the trial was withdrawn*, and Isaac was unharmed. The nearest way to the end of a tribulation is to be resigned to it. God cannot help you when you can bear a trial yourself. Give up all, and you shall keep all. Give up your Isaac, and Isaac shall not need to be given up. But if you will save your life, you shall lose it (Matt. 16:25).

Second, Abraham had the *expressed approval of God*: "for now I know that thou fearest God" (Gen. 22:12). The man whose conscience bears witness with the Holy Spirit enjoys great peace, and that peace comes to him because under trial he has proven himself true and faithful. And if we cannot stand the trials of this life, what shall we do in the day of judgment? If in the daily scales held in the hand of Providence we are found lacking, what shall we do before that great white throne where every thought shall be brought into judgment before the Most High?

Abraham next had *a clearer view of Christ than he ever had before*—no small reward. Jesus said, "Abraham rejoiced to see my day: and he saw it, and was glad" (John 8:56). In himself being ready to sacrifice his son, he had a representation of Jehovah who spared not His own Son. In the ram slaughtered instead of Isaac, he had a representation of the great Substitute who died that men might live.

More than that, to Abraham *God's name was more fully revealed that day*. He called Him Jehovah-jireh, a step in advance of anything that Abraham had known before. "If any man will do his will, he shall know of the doctrine" (John 7:17). The more you can stand the test of trial, the better instructed you shall be in the things of God. There is light beyond if you have grace to press through the difficulty.

To Abraham that day *the covenant was confirmed by oath*. The Lord swore by Himself (Gen. 22:16). You shall never get the grace of God so confirmed to you as when you have proven your fidelity to God by obeying him at all risks. You will then find how true the promises are, how faithful God is to the covenant of grace. The quickest road to full assurance is perfect obedience. While assurance will help you to obey, obedience will help you to be assured. "If ye keep my commandments, ye shall abide in my love; even as I have kept my Father's commandments, and abide in his love" (John 15:10).

Then it was that Abraham had also *a fuller promise with regard to the seed*. Out of the promises that Abraham received (Gen. 22:17–18), the first are mainly about the land, but the last are concerning his seed only. We get to love Christ more, to value Him more, to see Him, and to understand Him better, the more we are consecrated to the Lord's will.

And last of all, God pronounced over Abraham's head *a blessing*—a spectacular blessing so distinct and personal that it had never been given before and has not been repeated again to a man. Read it in Genesis 22:18. "In thy seed shall all the nations of the earth be blessed." First in trial, first in blessing. First in faithfulness to his God, Abraham becomes first in the sweet rewards that faithfulness is to obtain.

Let us ask God to make us like Abraham. May He help us to surrender those things in our hearts that we have as dear objects of affection. May we take all to the altar in our willingness to give all up, if the Lord wills. May we feel the spirit of perfect faith, believing that God's promises must be kept though outward circumstances and inward feelings should seem to contradict the Word of God. Let us labor to know the reality of faith. May we never pause to ask whether this shall make us rich or poor, honorable or despised, whether this will bring us peace or anguish, but let us go onward as though God had shot us from the eternal bow. Let us go right on in the full conviction that if there is temporary darkness, it must end in everlasting light. If there is present loss, it must end in eternal gain. Let us set our seal that in the end it must be our highest gain to serve God though that service should bring with it direful loss for the present.

Never sell your birthright for the world's wretched pottage. If our church were filled with men and women of faith, London would shake beneath the tramp of our army. The nation would perceive that a new power had arisen in the land, truth and righteousness would exalt their horn on high. Deceitful trading, greed for gold, and false religion would be put to an end once for all. Oh, that the flag of truth and righteousness might be unfurled by a valiant band, for that banner shall wave in the day of the last triumph when the banners of earth shall be rolled in blood. May the Lord make us true men like Abraham—true because believing—and may He help us to sacrifice our all for Jesus' sake.